JF

WRITERS ON FILE

General Editor: Simon Trussler
Associate Editor: Malcolm Page

D0103669

ARDEN
on File

Compiled by Malcolm Page

Methuen. London and New York

First published in 1985 in
simultaneous hardback and paperback editions
by Methuen London Ltd,
11 New Fetter Lane, London EC4P 4EE
and Methuen Inc, 733 Third Avenue,
New York, NY 10017

Typeset in IBM 9pt Press Roman
by ⴕ Tek-Art, Croydon, Surrey
Printed in Great Britain by Hazell Watson & Viney Ltd
Member of the BPCC Group
Aylesbury, Bucks

British Library Cataloguing in Publication Data

Page, Malcolm
    Arden on file.—(Writers on file)
    1. Arden, John—Criticism and interpretation
    I. Title   II. Series
    822'.914   PR6051.R3Z/

    ISBN 0-413-58500-X
    ISBN 0-413-56280-8 Pbk

822.914

A676

221298

Contents

7.95

The theatre is, by its nature, an ephemeral art: yet it is a daunting task to track down the newspaper reviews, or contemporary statements from the writer or his director, which are often all that remain to help us recreate some sense of what a particular production was like. This series is therefore intended to make readily available a selection of the comments that the critics made about the plays of leading modern dramatists at the time of their production — and to trace, too, the course of each writer's own views about his work and his world.

Many of these comments, together with factual information about first performances, major revivals, and publication details, are assembled in Section 2, on the plays themselves, which are arranged chronologically in order of their composition. Section 4, 'The Writer on His Work', brings together other comments from the playwright himself, dealing with more general matters of construction, opinion, or artistic development (the items here being arranged either chronologically or thematically, as suits the author and the material).

In addition to providing a uniquely convenient source of *documentation*, the 'Writers on File' series also assembles the *information* necessary for each reader to pursue further his interest in a particular writer or work. Thus, Section 1, 'A Brief Chronology', provides a quick, conspective overview of each playwright's life and career, while Section 3 offers concise guidance to the writer's own work in non-dramatic forms, and Section 5 provides a bibliographical guide to other primary and secondary sources of further reading.

Full details will be found in these latter sections of any sources otherwise cited under short-titles; but it should be noted that only collected editions of plays are included in the 'Select Bibliography', since publication details of individual titles are included with the other factual data on each play. A short synopsis of each play immediately follows this information, and for quick reference this is set in slightly larger, italic type.

The 'Writers on File' series hopes by striking this kind of balance between information and a wide range of opinion to offer 'companions' to the study of major playwrights in the international repertoire — not in that dangerously predigested fashion which can too readily quench the desire to read the plays themselves, nor so

General Editor's Introduction

5

prescriptively as to allow any single line of approach to predominate. Rather, the student users are encouraged to form their own judgements of the plays, to set against the many views here represented.

While we have tried to arrive at a format for the series which will enable users of one volume to find their way easily around any other, we recognize that some writers are, for example, far readier than others to talk about their own work. Others may, simply, be so prolific that it is not possible to present as full a range of critical opinion for each of their plays. And, of course — for reasons which do not necessarily have anything to do with intrinsic merits — some writers just attract a great deal more critical attention than others. For all these kinds of reasons, the compilers have been given the freedom to allow the particular qualities of their subjects, and of the critical response attracted, to dictate the precise presentation of the 'sampling' they have provided.

In the particular case of John Arden, there is the added consideration that an author whose early work was for traditional theatres and their audiences has made a conscious decision to look for alternative outlets for his work — a decision itself reflecting the development of his social and political thinking. Moreover, Arden provides a classic example of an author whose early plays have now achieved a respectable 'set-text' status — yet who was accorded very little recognition by any but the most perceptive critics at the time of their writing.

Here, then, the compiler has been concerned to reflect the process by which Arden has arrived at his present position in (or, more precisely, distance from) the conventional theatre scene. Particularly helpful is the full information about his lesser-known later plays (many of them, significantly, for radio) — as also the concisely-annotated bibliography of Arden's journalistic and other writings, through which the developments in his thinking traced in outline in the 'Writer on His Work' section can be followed more closely. It will be especially encouraging if those whose initial interest in this volume was as a study-aid to one of those 'set-text' plays were thus encouraged to discover the excitement and the range of the work in which, to borrow his own phrase, Arden has refused to 'do things properly'.

Simon Trussler

1930   26 Oct., born in Barnsley, West Yorkshire, son of the manager of a glass factory.

1935-39   Elementary school in Barnsley. 'It was impossible to live in such a town without being very conscious that one was a member of the minority party in the "class war." . . . A little boy going to school in the sort of nice clothes that my mother would provide, clean shirt and tie and polished shoes, was quite liable to get attacked in the street' (*The Playwrights Speak*, p.250-1).

1939-44   Preparatory school: 'They started us on Shakespeare when I was about nine' (*Theatre at Work*, p.37).

1944-48   Sedbergh School, a public school in Yorkshire: took English, French, and German for Higher School Certificate. Acted at school, including playing Hamlet, and wrote parts of five plays: 'all were approximately tragic in treatment, and all were in "costume"' ('A Thoroughly Romantic View', p.13). Occasionally saw plays in Sheffield and York.

1949-50   National Service as lance-corporal in Intelligence Corps (he describes his experiences in an essay in *All Bull*). Stationed for twelve months in Edinburgh Castle, a chance to see many plays.

1950-53   Read Architecture at King's College, Cambridge. 'Architecture was a professional training which I found interesting in itself, and which I could drop if I found my writing developing' (*Theatre at Work*, p.38).

1953-55   Completed training as architect at Edinburgh College of Art. College Theatre Group staged his first play, *All Fall Down* (unpublished), a comedy set in the Victorian period about building a railway. Also wrote 'a pseudo-Elizabethan tragedy on the Gunpowder Plot, . . . an unsatisfactory mixture of the Elizabethans and T.S. Eliot' (*Theatre at Work*, p.38).

1955-57   Worked in an architect's office in London, 'a large private office which was putting up a lot of those nasty office blocks that one sees: not a very ethical office, but a pleasant place to work as I liked the people' (*Theatre at Work*, p.38). *The Life of Man*, 90-minute unpublished radio play (broadcast by BBC, 16 Apr.

1956; won North Region new play prize), about ill-fated nine-teenth-century sailing-ship voyage, with allegorical overtones and influences including Ovid and John Masefield. George Devine of English Stage Company asked him for a play, rejecting the first (on Arthurian legends) and accepting *The Waters of Babylon* for one Sunday 'production without decor', 20 Oct. 1957, at the Royal Court Theatre. Married Margaretta D'Arcy, an Irish actress: they have four sons. Much of Arden's work from the mid-1960s in collaboration with her. Became a full-time writer at the end of the year.

1958 *When Is a Door Not a Door?*, short farce commissioned by Central School of Drama, London, and performed by students. *Live Like Pigs* at the Royal Court.

1959 Moved from London to near Peter Tavy, Devon, then to Brent Knoll, near Bristol. Bristol University Fellow in Playwriting for one year from Sept. *Serjeant Musgrave's Dance* performed at the Royal Court: awarded *Encyclopaedia Britannica* Prize.

1960 *Soldier, Soldier* televised by BBC, the first of his two TV plays. *The Happy Haven* (written with D'Arcy) at Bristol University, then at the Royal Court, the last of his plays to be staged there. Wrote a nativity play, *The Business of Good Government*, performed at Christmas in Brent Knoll church; D'Arcy directed and Arden played a Wise Man.

1961 *Wet Fish*, television play, transmitted by BBC. Founder-member of Committee of 100, to promote nuclear disarmament through civil disobedience (resigned after arrest and fine in Sept.). Moved to Full Sutton, village near York. Scripted *Top Deck*, 30-minute film made by David Andrews.

1962 Bought house on island in a lake in County Galway, Ireland: 'It is extremely difficult to get there – and very difficult for me to get off. I want it that way. I've done a lot of work there' (*The Playwrights Speak*, p.247). Wrote film script about Ned Kelly, commissioned by Karel Reisz, but never made.

1963 *The Workhouse Donkey*, rejected by the Royal Court, staged at Chichester Festival, Sussex, in its first year. *Ironhand* performed at Bristol Old Vic. Moved to the little town of Kirkbymoorside in North Yorkshire early in year, where he held in Aug. a well-publicized 'Festival of Anarchy' (based in his home). Says of his environs: 'I am perhaps more interested in a sort of historical or legendary approach to my work.... The Yorkshire countryside and also the Irish countryside, where I sometimes live, is conducive to this type of imagination' (*The Poet Speaks*, p.2). He says of his home life at this time: 'The family -- the children − are not supposed to come into [my] study. . . . Sometimes as a sort of treat I let some of them come in because they like to watch me write' (*The Playwrights Speak*, p.244).

1964 *Ars Longa, Vita Brevis*, short play, commissioned for fourteen- to seventeen-year-olds, written with D'Arcy, staged by Peter Brook in Royal Shakespeare Company's experimental *Theatre of Cruelty* season at LAMDA Theatre Club, London, and subsequently by D'Arcy with Kirkbymoorside Girl Guides. *Armstrong's Last Goodnight* performed in Glasgow. Presented *The Happy Haven* in Dublin, starring D'Arcy.

1965 *Armstrong's Last Goodnight* at Chichester Festival, transferring to National Theatre, London. *Left-Handed Liberty*, commissioned by the City of London to celebrate the 750th anniversary of the signing of Magna Carta, performed at Mermaid Theatre, London. Translated the spoken passages of Beethoven's opera *Fidelio* for Sadler's Wells Theatre. Arden has by now become a well-known dramatist and a critical success (though not a big commercial success), but from this point he turns more to fringe, minority, and regional activity.

1966 Left Kirkbymoorside and began dividing his time between a house in Muswell Hill, London, and County Galway. Became Chairman of *Peace News*, weekly pacifist paper, serving till 1970. *Friday's Hiding*, short experimental mime play, commissioned by Royal Lyceum Theatre, Edinburgh, and performed there. *The Royal Pardon*, a children's play, performed at Beaford Arts Centre, Devon, directed by Arden and D'Arcy, with Arden playing the Constable. *Serjeant Musgrave's Dance* successful in New York.

1967 Feb.-June: Visiting Professor in Humanities, New York University, where he staged an eleven-hour *Vietnam Carnival*, which he describes in 'Roll up Roll up to the Carnival of War', in *To Present the Pretence*.

1968 In June, *Harold Muggins Is a Martyr* presented by CAST (Cartoon Archetypical Slogan Theatre), with Arden and D'Arcy in cast, at Unity Theatre, London. Short play, *The True History of Squire Jonathan and his Unfortunate Treasure*, at Ambiance Lunch-Hour Theatre Club, London. *The Hero Rises Up* presented for four performances by Institute of Contemporary Arts at Roundhouse, London. Arden's new translation of Stravinsky's

Soldier's Tale performed at Bath Festival.

1970 *The Bagman* transmitted on BBC Radio in March. Arden and his family travelled in India for most of the year: Arden was ill with hepatitis, and they were imprisoned for a few days for attempting to enter Nagaland. He watched traditional dancing (describing this in 'The Chhau Dancers of Purulia' in *To Present the Pretence*), examined non-violent forms of action, considered writing a play about Gandhi, and began to consider more revolutionary answers to Third World problems (as he writes in the Preface to *Two Autobiographical Plays*).

1971 Settled in Corrandulla, County Galway, Ireland. Wrote, with D'Arcy and Roger Smith, *Two Hundred Years of Labour History*, for Socialist Labour League rally, Alexandra Palace, London, together with two short pieces for Muswell Hill Street Theatre, and *Rudi Dutschke Must Stay* for Writers against Repression.

1972 *The Ballygombeen Bequest* performed by 7:84 Company at Edinburgh Festival, Bush Theatre, London, and on tour. Ardens sued for a libel in the play, and case eventually settled out of court in Autumn 1977. *The Island of the Mighty* staged by the Royal Shakespeare Company at the Aldwych, London: during rehearsals, the Ardens protested that the play was being directed so as to appear in favour of imperialism, and picketed the theatre in protest. *Keep Those People Moving!*, a 40-minute nativity play, broadcast on schools' radio.

1973 Arden and D'Arcy Visiting Professors at the University of California, Davis, USA.

1975 *Non-Stop Connolly Show* presented complete in six parts in Dublin at Easter, lasting 26 hours. Parts of the cycle were then toured, and it was given a reading in fourteen instalments in London, May 1976. D'Arcy active with the Galway Theatre Workshop, with short political plays, from this time. Arden writer-in-residence at University of New England, Armidale, Australia, in late autumn.

1976 Arden and D'Arcy active in forming and shaping Theatre Writers' Group, later Theatre Writers' Union.

1977 *To Present the Pretence*, selected writings 1964-77, published.

1978 *Vandaleur's Folly* toured by the 7:84 Company. Radio play, *Pearl*, broadcast: won Giles Cooper Award as one of best radio plays of the year.

1979 *To Put it Frankly*, fifteen-minute radio play, broadcast. Occasional book and theatre reviewing in *New Statesman*.

1980 *The Adventures of the Ingenious Gentleman Don Quixote de la Mancha*, two-part radio adaptation of Cervantes' novel, broadcast.

1982 *Garland for a Hoar Head*, radio play about the sixteenth-century poet John Skelton, and *The Old Man Sleeps Alone*, 'a legend for radio of the building of Durham Cathedral', broadcast. *Silence among the Weapons*, his first novel, published: nominated for the Booker Prize. 'D'Arcy and I have been commissioned to write a series of BBC radio plays on early Christianity: maybe five, starting with the life of Christ and going through to Christianity's recognition by Constantine' (quoted in Michael Billington, 'The Drama Takes a Novel Turn', *Guardian,* 26 Aug. 1982, p.8).

1984 *The Manchester Enthusiasts*, two-part radio play, broadcast.

The Waters of Babylon

Play in three acts.

First London production: as one-night 'production without decor', Royal Court Th., 20 Oct. 1957 (dir. Graham Evans; with Robert Stephens as Krank).

First American production: Washington Th. Club, Apr. 1967.

Published: in *Three Plays.*

The central figure is Krank, a Pole, pimp, and slum-landlord in North London, and an architect, losing his job as the action unfolds. Paul, a Polish patriot, plans to kill the Russian leaders Khrushchev and Bulganin on their visit to England and demands the use of Krank's house to make the bomb. Krank refuses, so Paul asks for £500 instead. To raise this, Krank seeks the help of Butterthwaite, a shady Yorkshireman, who devises a lottery, sponsored by Joe Caligula, an incorruptible West Indian councillor. Krank meets Caligula at Speakers' Corner, Hyde Park, where he listens to a fatuous Tory MP and to the furtive, hysterically anti-foreign Henry Ginger. Both men suspect Paul and Krank are plotting against the Russian visitors. Ginger decides to spy on them, and the MP asks his mistress, Teresa (previously Krank's mistress), to assist. Teresa proves to be the long-lost sister of Cassidy, Krank's assistant. Caligula is enticed with an odd chant by Bathsheba, a West Indian prostitute. Then Ginger finds that Krank, who claimed to be a concentration-camp victim, was indeed at Buchenwald – in the German army. Krank and Butterthwaite scheme that the successful lottery ticket shall be theirs, but muddle the plan. Caligula sees at this point that his colleague in the lottery scheme is also the notorious slum-landlord. Ginger has betrayed Paul's plot to the police, so Paul pursues him, but accidentally kills Krank instead. Butterthwaite leads them in singing a cheerful four-part round. Arden describes the play as part of 'a sort of North Country tetralogy' with Soldier, Soldier, Wet Fish, *and* The Workhouse Donkey: 'I've just,* *slightly inconsistently, mixed the same characters through four plays' ('Arden of Chichester', p.17).*

I wrote *The Waters of Babylon* as a kind of cross-breed between two Elizabethan pieces — Jonson's *Alchemist* and Chapman's *Blind Beggar of Alexandria*. I wished to treat the complex international life of Notting Hill in terms of traditional comedy.

Arden, 'A Thoroughly Romantic View', p.14

One of the characters was drawn from life but the story of the play was invention. It was partly, of course, a satire on Macmillan's Premium Bond Scheme which came in at that time.

Arden, *Theatre at Work*, p.39

In *The Waters of Babylon,* where I used a lot of verse, I felt on re-reading it that many of the scenes would have been better if I had gone about them more naturalistically, and used a more natural prose.

Arden, *Theatre at Work*, p.42

The general theme — immigrants corrupted by life in Britain — is obscured by over-illustration. A mound of eccentric details, including an entire sub-plot set in an architects' office, stands between us and the author's meaning. In a wholly realistic play this would not matter so much, but Mr. Arden's piece (like certain novels by Miss Murdoch and Mr. Wain) is on the fringe of fantasy throughout; and when an author takes us into no-man's-land we are entitled to ask for signposts.

Kenneth Tynan, 'The Ego Triumphant',
The Observer, 27 Oct. 1957

An odd sort of farce-parable-extravaganza. . . . It seemed that Mr. Arden must have had a point to make — nobody brings references to Buchenwald and Auschwitz into a play just for the fun of it — but what that point is I have not the faintest idea. . . . The whole thing was pleasantly acceptable as an evening of zany, good-natured high jinks, rather like *The Hostage,* only not so good. (But I wonder what on earth Mr. Arden really had in mind?)

Julius Novick, *Beyond Broadway*
(New York: Hill and Wang, 1968), p.52

Probably the first entirely Brechtian play in the language.

Simon Trussler, 'The Book of the Play',
Tribune, 5 Feb. 1965

The Waters of Babylon is precisely about the difficulty of knowing who people are, and of making obvious judgements. Are we involved, asks Arden, with tragedy or farce: with play-acting or truth: with games or reality? And is it possible to separate these categories?

Albert Hunt, *Arden*, p.44-5

The technical skill of the piece is at times stronger than its release of resultant energies into fruitful channels: but for a first play it remains a considerable achievement in its complete independence of manner and in its control over its own density of matter.

Simon Trussler, *John Arden*, p.9

When Is a Door Not a Door?

'An industrial episode' in one act.
First London production: by Central School of Drama, Embassy Th., Swiss Cottage, 2 June 1958.
Published: in *Soldier, Soldier, and Other Plays.*

During one morning in a factory office, a strike starts, personalities clash, work contrasts with pointless bustle, the gap between office staff and workers is shown, and through all this two workmen proceed with removing and replacing a door.

Commissioned by Central School, to provide eleven parts of roughly equal size, and written and staged within a month, Arden thought the play 'completely realistic' until the director gave it the style of 'a kind of *commedia dell'arte* fantasy'. 'I enjoyed writing it, however, as a purely technical exercise, and I enjoyed seeing them do it.'

Arden, 'Preface', *Soldier, Soldier, and Other Plays*, p.11-12

Live Like Pigs

Play in seventeen scenes.

First London production: Royal Court Th., 30 Sept. 1958 (dir.
George Devine and Anthony Page; with Wilfred Lawson as
Sailor Sawney, Anna Manahan as Rachel, Robert Shaw as
Blackmouth, Nigel Davenport as Mr. Jackson, and Margaretta
D'Arcy as Rosie).

First New York production: Th. Company of Boston, at Actors'
Playhouse, 7 June 1965.

Paris production: Centre Dramatique National 'La Guilde',
Tep-Maison de la Culture, 19 Oct. 1966 (fully documented in
Les Voies de la création théâtrale, 5, ed. Denis Bablet and Jean
Jacquot, Paris: Ed. du Centre National de la Recherche
Scientifique, 1977, p.345-76).

Revived: Th. Upstairs, London, 4 Feb. 1972 (dir. Pam Brighton).

Published: in *New English Dramatists,* 3, ed. Tom Maschler
(Penguin, 1961); and in *Three Plays.*

*A group of wanderers, the Sawneys, 'descendants of the "sturdy
beggars" of the sixteenth century', are rehoused on a council
estate. They include Sailor, a tough old drunkard, who lives with
Rachel, 'a tall handsome termagant'; Rosie, a tired, sullen woman
with two children; a loutish teenager Col, with 'swift and violent
mannerisms', Blackmouth, half-gypsy and an escaped convict; Old
Croaker, 'a batty old hag, alternately skittish and comatose';
and her strange, sick daughter Daffodil, with 'an old, old face like
that of a malicious fairy'. From the start they 'live like pigs',
neglecting the house and snubbing the doctor and official from
the Housing Department. Next door live the conventional
Jacksons, 'undistinguished but not contemptible', who soon
quarrel with the Sawneys. Old Croaker steals their washing, Col
assaults their daughter, Mr. Jackson sleeps with Rachel, and then
is angered by her. Finally Col is attacked by a mob which besieges
the house, and police plan to evict the occupants. Sailor is injured,
and Col, Daffodil, and Rachel run away, leaving Old Croaker and
Sally chanting a spell to protect them.*

Live Like Pigs was based on something which happened in Barnsley
some years before, when a council house was given to a family of

15

squatters. I didn't find out too many actual details, because I didn't want to be stuck too closely to a documentary form, but it was a similar situation, and certainly ended up like *Live Like Pigs*, with the house being besieged by the neighbours.

Arden, *Theatre at Work,* p.39-40

When I wrote this play I intended it to be not so much a social document as a study of differing ways of life brought sharply into conflict and both losing their own particular virtues under the stress of intolerance and misunderstanding. In other words, I was more concerned with the 'poetic' than the 'journalistic' structure of the play. . . . I approve outright neither of the Sawneys nor of the Jacksons. Both groups uphold standards of conduct that are incompatible, but which are both valid in their correct context. . . . The play is in large part meant to be funny.

Arden, 'Introductory Note', *Three Plays,* p.101

Live Like Pigs is a dramatization by John Arden of the popular theory that the Welfare State destroys splendid individualism. . . . I am all for people living in their own way. The characters in *The Lower Depths* do just that. But Gorki avoided Mr. Arden's mistake, which is to see the world outside as a world of stuffy, small-souled hypocrites, inferior simply *because* they are ordinary.

Kenneth Tynan, 'A World Fit for Eros',
The Observer, 5 Oct. 1958

No one in his right mind would go to *Live Like Pigs* for pleasure. . . . We simply wallow in the filth of a bunch of boozy, lecherous, dishonest tramps. . . . In spite of its incredibilities (where were the council officials, where the other neighbours?) and the maddening sandwiching of its many scenes with dreadful doggerel ballads, *Live Like Pigs* is powerful. But so is any cartload of manure.

Eric Keown, 'At the Play', *Punch,* 8 Nov. 1958

What *Live Like Pigs* reveals is an exciting, formidable talent for putting flesh-and-blood people on the stage with a racy, poetic turbulent vitality that recalls Mr. Arden's Elizabethan models. Breaking through the class-barrier, he also breaks open genteel conventions about language and love on the stage for the underprivileged.

Richard Findlater, *'Live Like Pigs'*, *The Encore Reader,*
ed. Charles Marowitz, Tom Milne, and Owen Hale
(Methuen, 1965), p.93

Suddenly, Arden has found absolute clarity of focus and consistency of style. For the first time, he's a master of his material. ... It's a big and pleasant surprise that Arden manages to bring so many different characters so vividly to life, differentiating so well between them. ... The pace is rapid, the texture is thick, and the incidents are varied.

Ronald Hayman, *John Arden* (Heinemann, 1969), p.14-17

It is a boisterous, driving outburst of human spirit under compression, it plays like a roller coaster — swooping and diving and screaming at the tight corners.

Robert Hatch, 'Arden' *Nation* (New York), 21 June 1965

Live Like Pigs can now be seen as one of the best plays of the 'fifties. ... Pam Brighton's production misses no details, physical or dramatic, and bounds along with great assurance, taking the scraps of ballad unselfconsciously in its stride.

Derek Mahon, 'The Good Life', *The Listener*, 17 Feb. 1972

What impresses about *Live Like Pigs* is not the fact that it is perhaps the earliest British play to attack the dehumanizing potential of the welfare state, or to incorporate Brecht-type songs within a naturalistic structure, but that it survives in performance as a warm-blooded, undogmatic, and beautifully-written piece of theatre. ... If the play's overall movement is grim and minatory, Arden paints his individual characters and events with great humorous detail. ... The darker side of the play — built principally round Blackmouth's return to claim his wife and child, but extending into the broader theme of officialdom's stubborn misguided attempts to regiment the social misfit — is given equal value in Pam Brighton's production. The songs prove especially effective in this respect, signalling mood changes from the comic to the serious, and releasing emotions built up in Arden's abrasively naturalistic dialogue. What prevents the play from ever becoming a simplistic socialist tract is Arden's ability to

illustrate that not all the blame lies in the social conditions. However aggravated they are by the bureaucratic pedantry of the
welfare state, the Sawneys have a built-in self-destructiveness
which would vitiate their life together in any environment.

Nigel Andrews, *'Live Like Pigs'*, *Plays and Players*, Apr. 1972

Serjeant Musgrave's Dance

'An un-historical parable' in three acts.

First London production: Royal Court Th., 22 Oct. 1959 (dir.
Lindsay Anderson; with Ian Bannen as Musgrave, Frank Finlay
as Attercliffe, and Freda Jackson as Mrs. Hitchcock).

First New York production: Th. de Lys, 8 Mar. 1966.

Revived: Royal Court Th., 9 Dec. 1965 (dir. Jane Howell; with
Iain Cuthbertson as Musgrave); CSC Repertory, New York,
Dec. 1977; National Th. at Cottesloe Th., 27 May 1981 (dir.
John Burgess; with John Thaw as Musgrave); Old Vic, 22 May
1984 (dir. Albert Finney who also played Musgrave).

Published: Plays and Players, Sept. and Oct. 1961; London:
Methuen, 1960; Methuen Student Edition, ed. Glenda
Leeming, 1982; and in *Plays One*.

*'Set in a mining town in the north of England' during a cold
winter, 1860-80. Four soldiers arrive, ostensibly recruiting: the
stern, religious Serjeant Musgrave; middle-aged Attercliffe; moody,
handsome Hurst; and cheerful young Sparky. Brought to the
town by the sinister Bargee, they billet at the inn run by the
tough, kindly Mrs. Hitchcock, whose barmaid, Annie, has lost her
lover, Billy Hicks, who joined the army and was killed in a
colonial war. The miners, led by Walsh, are on strike, and the
Mayor, with his cronies the Parson and the Constable, are hoping
that the soldiers will recruit the strike leaders. Annie comes to the
three soldiers and plans to run away with Sparky. Attercliffe tries
to stop them and accidentally kills Sparky. Next morning the
remaining soldiers hold the recruiting meeting in the market-place:
instead, Musgrave explains that he and Attercliffe took part in the
round-up in the colony which followed Hicks's death: five
innocent people were killed. Now they have brought 'wildwood
madness' to the town 'to work that guilt back to where it began'.
Pointing their Gatling gun at the crowd, Musgrave says that 25 of*

them are needed to work out his 'Logic' – for 'we've got to be remembered!' He hoists the skeleton of Hicks and dances beneath it. Then dragoons, summoned from a nearby town, enter: Hurst is shot and the others arrested. The townspeople dance in a circle round Annie, cradling Hicks's skeleton. Arden explains what the text's directions omit: 'The audience should be made conscious of the fact that the town has been taken over by the real military – the dragoons. . . . In a larger theatre, . . . the stage would be full of dragoons and the dance would take place in front of them. . . . Even the most sympathetic of the colliers, who nearly sides with Musgrave, has no alternative but to take part in the dance' (Theatre at Work, *p.45). In the last scene, Musgrave and Attercliffe, in prison awaiting execution, are visited by Mrs. Hitchcock. Attercliffe has learned that 'you can't cure the pox by further whoring', and has the last line: 'D'you reckon we can start an orchard?'*

The first idea for the play came to me in stage terms partly because of its spectacle. I had seen a number of contemporary plays and felt – particularly with *Live Like Pigs* – well, this is all very nice, I like this play, but I can see, looking at it on the stage, why some people don't like it. It *is* grey. And I suddenly wanted to write a play with a visual excitement as well as a verbal one. I visualized the stage full of scarlet uniforms.

Arden, 'Building the Play', *Encore,* July-Aug. 1961, p.40

I wrote it rather rapidly, all sort of on fire with an idea. . . . Really successful plays come out of a fusion of the imagination and the intellect. And in this particular case, I think the imagination was on fire when I wrote the play but my intellect was somewhat in abeyance.

Arden, interviewed by Ira Peck,
New York Times, 10 Apr. 1966, Sec. II, p.3

I used my historical imagination, and decided that the most likely character would be one of those Crimean sergeants, who fought with a rifle in one hand, and bible in the other.

Arden, *Theatre at Work,* p.44

I started off with the first scene complete – four men on a canal bank, waiting for a barge, one of them making jokes. This automatically puts [Sparky] into a sort of isolation – if he is making jokes all the time there must be a failure in communication between him and everybody else. Because you cannot carry on a complete relationship in the form of jokes.

Arden, 'Building the Play', p.39

[The Mayor and Parson are 'silhouettes'.] What I've done is take a character – if you like, a nineteenth-century coalowner who's also the mayor of a small town, and simply drawn him in very simple lines so that only the parts of his character that are important to the play are seen. . . . I've purely emphasized in the Mayor those aspects of the man's character that deal with his attitude to the coal industry and his attitude to the military.

Arden, 'Arden of Chichester', p.18

The basic image of the British soldier, I think, is not Tommy in Khaki, but a toy soldier in a scarlet coat, which is still worn outside Buckingham Palace. It also turned out very convenient for various other reasons. It enabled me to use a Victorian ballad tradition for the imagery and so on. And it was quite a suitable period, being of naked rather than apologetic imperialism.

'John Arden, interviewed by Brendan Hennessy',
Transatlantic Review, No.40, Summer 1971. p.56

One of the things that set the play off was an incident in Cyprus [in Famagusta, 3 Oct. 1958]. A soldier's wife was shot in the street by terrorists. And according to newspaper reports – which was all I had to work on at the time – some soldiers ran wild at night and people were killed in the rounding-up. The atrocity which sparks off Musgrave's revolt, and which happens before the play begins, is roughly similar.

Interviewers: In the Cyprus incident, five people died, one of them a little girl, as in your play.

Arden: That was quite deliberate.

Arden, Theatre at Work, p.44

[In the Army] I heard some sort of hair-raising stories about things that were done by British soldiers during World War II which never got into the papers. And I was interested in the attitudes expressed by men who'd had experience with these things. Some soldiers were quite callous about it. Others had sort of a permanent guilty conscience and were still disturbed by it. That is really what I wanted to show in the play — what would happen to soldiers who are reasonable, decent, garden variety servicemen if they became so upset by something they had done that they couldn't stick in the army any longer.

Arden, interviewed by Ira Peck, p.3

I did not fully understand my own feelings about pacifism until I wrote *Serjeant Musgrave*: nor about old age until I wrote *The Happy Haven*.

Arden, *Theatre at Work*, p.46

I have not managed to balance the business of giving the audience information so that they can understand the play with the business of witholding information in order to keep the tension going.

Arden, interviewed by Walter Wager,
'Who's for a Revolution?', *Tulane Drama Review*,
Winter 1966, p.42

The general purpose of the soldiers' visit should be made much clearer. The real trouble is that in the churchyard scene, where they explain themselves, there is a tremendous amount of emotion being generated. They are all getting angry with each other, and Musgrave goes off into a religious tirade. The result is that the audience is so busy watching the actors dramatizing their emotions that they aren't picking up the plot information which is being conveyed in the dialogue.

Arden, *Theatre at Work*, p.48

I think what I was doing in *Musgrave* was using two acts for what is commonly done in one, in most three-act plays. I don't see that this is necessarily wrong.

Arden, *Theatre at Work*, p.39

The actual shape of the play and the overall meaning of it seem to me now to be muddled. . . . It was a play about soldiers and about the relationship of the soldier to the community. And it's this relationship that's muffled. Musgrave has a lot to say about it, and so do the others, but they don't actually get their teeth into it and worry it out enough. There just isn't enough hard thinking in the last third of the play.

Arden, interviewed by Brendan Hennessy, p.55

Protest is a sort of futile activity in the theatre. . . . It's highly unlikely, for instance, that supposing President Johnson and Mr. McNamara came to see this play, they would say, 'Oh dear, we've got to pull out of Vietnam'. It's also unlikely that the couple of hundred people in the Theater de Lys are going to suddenly get up and rush out of the theatre and start a revolution. So that if you write a play that is protesting against something, you are putting yourself in a position of frustration from the very beginning. . . . Yet I think it's very necessary that it should be done. . . . The only thing you can do is to keep on saying what you don't like about the society in which you live, so that even if the forces that one objects to, in this case the forces that are continuing the wars of the world, even if they finally win and we do have another world war, one will at least be able to say, 'Well, I did get up and say no before it was too late'.

Arden, interviewed by Ira Peck, p.3

Please don't attach too much weight to the drama critic of *The Times* who says 'When [this play] first appeared, its sidelong references to the Cyprus troubles over-shadowed the main content. . . . The action has now settled into legend.' Cyprus may be a solved problem. May be. Aden? Malaysia? Do I have to list them? Rhodesia was once a Victorian Imperialist adventure. Vietnam has never been a *British* colony, of course, but . . . 1965-66 is as ugly a year's end as was 1958-59, when this play was conceived and written. I propose to give all my royalties from this production to the Christian Action funds for relief of political prisoners in South Africa. Because South Africa is the worst reminder we have of those historical grandfathers of ours who sent the 'legendary' Serjeant Musgrave and his men off to the wars.

Arden, programme note to 1965 revival, Royal Court Theatre

It was apparent to me on my recent visit to New York that many people are puzzled by this play. By unhappy coincidence rather than by any prophetic powers of mine, the play turns out to be directly relevant to the Vietnam situation, which presents Americans with many of the same problems that Englishmen had to face in connection with Cyprus in 1959. If Serjeant Musgrave fails in his attempt to bring the war to an end, it is not because I believe such an attempt to be objectively impossible. Indeed I believe it is not only possible but mandatory for citizens in a democracy to use their voices in this cause. The play shows the difficulties involved. They are very great. I myself, alone, do not pretend to be able to solve them. Wars are made by democracies in the name of peace. This I find more sickening than the acts of unashamed aggressors. Our society claims certain virtues. We must act — all of us, as individuals, and en masse — as though the claim is true. One man shouting 'No' gets nowhere — millions, whispering it, with diffidence and even with timidity, can make a noise like a tornado. If, at the same time, they act upon that one small word, they will have won.

> Arden, advertisement in *New York Times*,
> 15 May 1966, Sec. 2, p.4

I wrote a play attacking the complacency with which the British public was prepared to regard actions undertaken by the British Army in foreign parts. The play becomes famous. It is presented as an examination piece for schoolchildren. And the British Army continues to do exactly the same things in Ireland, and has been doing so for ten years.

> Arden, interviewed by Ronald Hayman,
> 'Art Values', *The Listener*, 4 Sept. 1980

Another frightful ordeal. It is time someone reminded our advanced dramatists that the principal function of the theatre is to give pleasure. . . . It is the duty of the theatre, not to make men better, but to render them harmlessly happy.

> Harold Hobson, *Sunday Times*, 25 Oct. 1959

Why was this piece put on? A play that was anti-Empire and anti-Army would conceivably have its appeal in Sloane Square, but surely not one that was eighty years out of date? If a tract was wanted on those lines it could have been written more persuasively by an intelligent child. . . . There might have been some felicities of dialogue or wit to leaven this lump of absurdity, but

23

I failed to detect them.

Eric Keown, 'At the Play', *Punch*, 28 Oct. 1959

I have never seen a play which created its own mad, obsessed, other-world so completely as *Serjeant Musgrave's Dance*. Partly this is due to the nightmare draughtsmanship of the designer Jocelyn Herbert. Miss Herbert's world is half Ackerman print, half German silent film — remote, yet alive, in the centre of one of those crystal balls which foam into a snowstorm when you turn them upside down. Her patterns are black and white in sepia lit by blotches of colour. The scarlet uniforms, the shining rifles, the warm brown bar counter, the heavy dark trunks are all solid and three-dimensional, but outside and around them is wrapped the thick white blanket of winter. . . .

The characters' reactions have always to be several sizes too large for their actions. The mention of a man's name in a pub resounds like a cannonade. The drop of a trunk on a quayside starts off tremors of an earthquake. The hoisting of a skeleton to a flagpole is expected to change the world. Mr. Anderson [the director] accepts the melodrama and even underlines and emphasizes it in the style of a UFA thriller. He uses an eerie warbling note like that of a musical saw to rivet our attention to the insanity hovering above his characters. A sepulchral dissonant organ march [by Dudley Moore] ushers in the acts. These are all, in a sense, Irvingesque devices more fitted to the Lyceum than to the Court. But, amazingly, they work.'

Alan Brien, 'Disease of Violence', *Spectator*, 30 Oct. 1959

There is no conflict. The soldiers and the colliers, the bargee and the barmaid being all against the army and so basically of the same mind, the playwright seems to have gone to some pains to remove any possible cause of disagreement between them. Yet they are undeniably up against each other. I defy anyone to explain the plot, except perhaps as a series of expedients to stave off the grand climax until the last act; even then, to understand may be to forgive but it does not make it any easier to connect. It is all the more aggravating since Mr. Arden has a genius for bold theatrical effects, which we cannot get from anyone else and which he throws away. . . . Muddle runs through the whole play and by the end has reached truly startling proportions: Musgrave holds up the town at gunpoint in the market place. Why? What does he hope to gain by it? What is the crowd supposed to do if they wish to surrender to him? By this time the way behind is so strewn with red herrings that who can tell?

Hilary Spurling, 'Royal Fortress', *Spectator*, 17 Dec. 1965

What goes wrong with the play is a technical gamble in construction. Sparky's stabbing by his infuriated co-deserter Hurst is the hinge of the plot, the accident which trips up Musgrave's scheme. [Arden] muffles the impact of Sparky's death with a flurry of melodramatic comings and goings. The gamble doesn't pay off. The play's sure flow is dislocated, and with it, more seriously, its sense of reality. Everything that happens up to that point has had the profoundly rooted feel of growing cause and consequence. Sparky's death is turned into a non-event. There may be something, too, in the accusation that Arden dithers too long in his final working-out of the moral lesson of his play, the long scene in prison between the defeated Musgrave and the landlady who shows his his error. . . . It's a weakness of *Musgrave* that what commences with the power and sureness of a legend or ballad peters out in discussion.

Ronald Bryden, 'Deep as England', *The Unfinished Hero* (London: Faber, 1969), p.98-9

The Happy Haven

Written with Margaretta D'Arcy. Play in three acts (divided into two acts in earliest publication, 1962).
First production: Drama Studio, Bristol University, Apr. 1960.
First London production: Royal Court Th., 14 Sept. 1960 (dir. William Gaskill; with Peter Bowles as Copperthwaite, Rachel Roberts as Mrs. Letouzel, and Frank Finlay as Crape).
First American productions: University Th. Group, Rhode Island University, 9 May 1963; Long Wharf Th., New Haven, 1966.
Published: in *New English Dramatists*, 4, ed. Tom Maschler (Penguin, 1962); and in *Three Plays*.

Dr. Copperthwaite, Superintendent of an old people's nursing home, has perfected an Elixir of Life which he intends to try out on the helplessly regimented inmates. They are at first exhilarated by the prospect, but are easily persuaded by one of their number, himself excluded from the experiment, that rejuvenation can only

ensure a repetition of the sufferings and frustrations from which old age has released them. They therefore contrive to inject Dr. Copperthwaite with a massive dose of his own medicine, and he reappears as a chubby schoolboy, clutching his teddy-bear, to perch grotesquely on the ecstatic knees of a baby-starved crone.
Jeremy Brooks, 'Most Likely to Succeed',
New Statesman, 24 Sept. 1960

[Between the first production in Bristol] and London I cut about half the images because I found that an actor with a mask does not need elaborate language — the mask is so powerful in itself that it needs a more naked expression of emotion. But I *am* simplifying my language in general as I go on writing, because I have come to the conclusion that elaborate verbiage on the stage tends to miss a lot of its effects simply because people haven't time to listen and watch at the same time.
Arden, *Theatre at Work,* p.42

When I began to work on *The Happy Haven,* I found it was developing into a grotesque comedy about an old folks' home ... and then when the theme seemed to be demanding more stylized treatment, it seemed a good idea to use masks on young actors and actresses. You can't have actors, like, say, Edith Evans and Sybil Thorndike in that sort of play, because they are too near the real age, and it becomes cruel in the wrong sense. And also, on a purely technical level, the older the actors the slower they go. If you are writing a comedy, this imposes problems.
Arden, *Theatre at Work,* p.41

The cast did achieve a breadth of style and a boldness of characterization they could never have achieved in make-up, however grotesque. The imagination *was* released by the mask, and for me absolutely justified the experiment.
William Gaskill, 'Comic Masks and *The Happy Haven*',
Encore, No.23 (Nov.-Dec. 1960), p.18

The Happy Haven is an essay, something much more stylish which derives largely from the classical comedy of the sixteenth century and the Italian commedia and a comedy of humours. ...

These are reputable theatrical conventions that have been going off and on for four or five hundred years. It seems to me that it is up to the critics to know about these things and to recognize them.

Arden, 'The Writer's View', *Contrast,* Winter 1962, p.133

The Doctor in *The Happy Haven* is a comic character in everything except his work. He is in fact a brilliant scientist and this gives him that element of the tragic; one must take him seriously on that level, otherwise the play doesn't make sense.

Arden, 'Arden of Chichester', p.16-17

[Arden] has moved on to the more brittle impersonality of *Paid on Both Sides, The Dance of Death,* and the Auden-Isherwood moralities. He uses the same trappings: grotesque masks and scientific paraphernalia, huge syringes, and huger babies, a farcical but knowing psychology, and, occasionally, bright galloping verse. The theme, too, is Audenesque: a fierce satire on the morality, or brutalization, of the scientific bureaucrats. . . .

Arden needs this hardness and impersonality. For people disgust him, they fill him with horror. The only human condition he really responds to is indignity. He hates the lot of them, the scientist and the crocks, with their grasping pettiness and pretensions, their self-absorption, their machinations and bowel-movements, their lusts, itches and brutalities.

A. Alvarez, 'New Experiments for Old',
New Statesman, 16 Apr. 1960

An elephantine comedy of humours. . . . Arden fails not merely because his wit is elephantine, but because his play has no anchor in normality. The characters are all unhinged, and there is no one to act as a bridge between ourselves and the grotesques across the footlights.

Kenneth Tynan, *A View of the English Stage*
(London: Davis-Poynter, 1975), p.278

The masks, besides defining the appropriate humour, also make the point that such attitudes are, literally, masks that have hardened with the years into a permanent shell over the natural features. . . . The setting gives the method a further justification.

It is a property of all closed institutions — barracks, hospital, prison, or residential hotel — to transform the inmates into types, even grotesque types. They are known to each other by ingrained behaviour patterns. . . . Just as the characters in a ballad can discharge a weight of direct emotion beyond the scope of romantic writing, Arden's masked ancients are able to reveal themselves with a simple expressiveness which attempted in any naturalistic idiom, would appear maudlin.

Irving Wardle, 'Live Like Guinea Pigs',
Encore, No.28 (Nov.-Dec. 1960), p.37

[Copperthwaite] is acting with the best intentions; he, too, is in the right according to his own standards, and really sees his new youth elixir as a benefit to mankind, even if, carried away by his fanaticism on this subject, he forgets to consider the feelings of the individual men and women in his charge. . . . He is not a two-dimensional stereotype representing some abstract concept, but a human being with certain standards: we can understand his problems, too, even if we do not necessarily approve of his reactions to them.

John Russell Taylor, Anger and After
(London: Methuen, 1969), p.97-9

The Business of Good Government

'A Christmas play', in one act.

First production: St Michael's Church, Brent Knoll, Somerset, Dec. 1960 (dir. Arden and D'Arcy; with Arden as Wise Man, and a local amateur cast).

Published: London: Methuen, 1963; re-issued 1983.

Arden noticed that the church at Brent Knoll would be very suitable for a play, as the chancel was raised four feet higher than the nave, with no screen, so he visited the vicar and offered to write a play, which largely follows the New Testament, in short scenes. Mary and Joseph come to the Bethlehem inn, the baby is born, angels summon Shepherds to visit them, the Wise Men visit Herod, and then Jesus, Joseph, Mary, and the baby flee to Egypt, closely followed by Herod, whose concern is with the demands of 'good government'.

The play is 'realist' in that the characters stand for themselves as Shepherds, Wise Men, Kings, and what have you, and are not intended to carry symbolical or psychological overtones. But it is also 'non-realist' in that the principal action is miraculous and accepted as such. This double level of interpretation should be reflected in the appearance of the characters.

Arden, 'Author's Preface',
The Business of Good Government, p.10

I saw Herod as an administrator, not exceptionally tyrannical in his approach to his job — which is blatantly unhistorical, because, in fact, Herod *was.* But in my play he finds himself in a corner and can see no other way out but to order the massacre.

Arden, *Theatre at Work,* p.47

The reactions of Arden's characters to the events of this most familiar of all stories are fresh, convincing, naturalistic. . . . The wise men are pedants, confident in their own astrology but lacking in imagination; they are visibly disappointed and puzzled by the humble scene which their brilliant reading of the stars has led them to. The innkeeper is a neurotic chatterbox. . . . At least one of the shepherds resents being disturbed in the middle of the night by an angel. . . . It is living characters, rather than phrase-ology, that can make an old tale new.

Bamber Gascoigne, 'Oh What a Lovely Ball',
The Observer, 29 Dec. 1963

It retains added interest as Arden's first attempt at a kind of community drama that has since preoccupied him: and as a printed script it fails only in disappointing the expectations it arouses of a fuller development of Herod's character — for the emphasis shifts. . . . It is a notable achievement that Arden can counterpoint the immediacy of such practical considerations — whether these arise from Herod's national interests or Joseph's pressing order book — with his spiritual theme. . . . The whole play resembles more an episode from a modern mystery cycle than a self-contained work.

Simon Trussler, *John Arden,* p.22-3

The Workhouse Donkey

'A vulgar melo-drama' in three acts, commissioned to be
performed by the English Stage Company during the opening
celebrations for Coventry Cathedral in May 1962, but rejected
by the Company.

First production: Chichester Festival, 8 July 1963 (dir. Stuart
Burge; with Frank Finlay as Butterthwaite and Robert
Stephens as Wiper).

Published: Plays and Players, Aug. and Sept. 1963; London:
Methuen, 1964; and in *Plays One.*

*The generously diffuse action relates the downfall of Charlie
Butterthwaite, a Labourite hero-villain. . . . Butterthwaite is the
Napoleon of the North, a man of power in a place not altogether
unlike the author's native town of Barnsley. . . . A plot of almost
Elizabethan complexity is touched off by the arrival of a new
Chief Constable, Colonel Feng, who is determined to uncover all
infractions of the law, in U [upper-class] circles as well as among
the cloth caps. So the petty Labour crime of meeting in a pub
after hours is found to be matched by petty Tory vice in a night
club with a meaty side-line. [Finally Butterthwaite robs] the
Borough Treasurer's safe; he is caught, disgraced and thrust back
into the outer darkness from which he had emerged after years of
struggle. Once again he becomes, not the all-powerful kingpin in
local politics, but the Workhouse Donkey, the victim of a class
system loaded against him from the start. And in the end our
sympathy is with the old rascal.*

G.W. Brandt, *'The Workhouse Donkey',*
New Theatre Magazine (Bristol), V, 2 (1964), p.41

The Workhouse Donkey I would regard as a straightforward
classical comedy in structure. It's based on the sort of Jonsonian
type of comedy in which you get a fairly large cast, a contemporary theme with social comment in it, and then an elaboration of
plot which is not realistic but fantastic, ending up in a sort of
classical shape to the play – you know, the various threads of the
plot culminating in a big scene at the end, for instance, in which
everybody's exposed, and the use of verse to give an extra dimension to the goings-on. I'm also using some shreds from English

music-hall and pantomime tradition, which are more apparent when the play's staged than when you read it.

Arden, 'Arden of Chichester', p.18

I wanted to set on the stage the politics, scandals, sex life, and atmosphere of Barnsley, as I remembered shocked Conservative elders talking about it in my youth. . . . Many of the characters are taken from life. Certain key incidents − the burglary at the town hall, the incident at the *Victoria*, the politics of the art gallery, and so on − belong in a not-so-veiled form to the politics of Barnsley. The chief constable controversy is based upon a row they had in Nottingham a few years ago [1959].

Arden, *Theatre at Work*, p.51

I feel that [Feng] is a good man who behaves in a way dictated by feelings of the utmost integrity, and concludes by doing a tremendous amount of damage. Whereas on the other hand Butterthwaite is a pretty scoundrelly sort of person, who nevertheless has had a guiding ideal in his life when he was a young man, which still sticks with him in a curious fashion. He still sees himself as representing the true spirit of socialism, but he has in fact forgotten what it really means, and is relishing just his personal power. But my view of Butterthwaite − this is a purely personal view − is that the type of municipal corruption that he represents does a great deal less harm to a community of people where it is understood and lived with than the type of ferocious integrity implied in the figure of the Chief Constable.

Arden, 'On Comedy', p.15

The view of the donkey I was thinking of in the play was the one that's expressed in Butterthwaite's song, of the donkey as an image expressing lust and anti-social behaviour and bad smells, generally rather a disgusting little animal, which is one of its attributes in mythological tradition. It's much more likely, I think, that I had in mind the Golden Ass of Apuleius than the specifically Christian story. And the old councillor is chucked out of the town as a sort of scapegoat. . . . Having been their king, he's then sacrificed and driven out, and will in turn be replaced by somebody else. . . . It's intended again to refer to the medieval character, the Lord of Misrule. This is what he has become.

Arden, 'On Comedy', p.13-14

31

I wanted . . . to deal with local personalities in a raucous Aristophanic manner that would develop a poetic intensity from its very looseness.

Arden, *Theatre at Work*, p.51

[The play] left me feeling it was after all possible to unite passion, politics, poetry, sex, and song in a living theatrical form. Brought up as a child on Stratfordian Shakespeare on the one hand and Midlands music hall on the other, I had often longed for a work that would fuse the two traditions; and in Arden's masterpiece I felt I had at last found it. . . . This is a work that needs to be felt on the senses rather than read in the study. Moreover it needs, I suspect, to be seen in the kind of close-knit, rough-hewn community where it is set. . . . The play is not just a kaleidoscopic portrait of a living community; it also has the moral uncertainty of life itself.

Michael Billington, 'Donkey Serenade',
The Guardian, 20 May 1975

Ironhand

Play in three acts, 'adapted from Goethe's *Goetz von
   Berlichingen*'.
First production: Bristol Old Vic, 12 Nov. 1963 (dir. Val May;
   with Christopher Benjamin as Goetz, and Sheila Allen).
Television production: BBC2, 11 Apr. 1965 (dir. Rudolph
   Cartier).
Published: London: Methuen, 1965.

*Ironhand is Goetz, who lost his right hand in battle and replaced
it with an iron gauntlet. He is a Free Knight, effectively independent and responsible only to a distant Emperor. But now, in the
early sixteenth century, higher authority can no longer tolerate
Goetz's robbery and violence. He seizes Weislingen, emissary of
the Bishop of Bamberg, and, after making an agreement with him
that is soon broken, robs a wagon-train. Besieged in his castle and
forced to surrender, he is treacherously arrested and dramatically
rescued during his trial. Blackmailed into leading a peasants'
revolt, the rebels soon turn against him, and he is captured. Weislingen plans to execute Goetz, but is persuaded to change his*

mind. Weislingen dies, poisoned; and, in the final scene, Goetz is in prison, his legs in irons. He too dies, crushed, saying: 'I stood by myself and I took no heed of nobody. All I said was freedom. All Weislingen said was some sort of order.'

It's an exciting play of medieval action, with a good deal of serious social and historical stuff in it, because it was written about a period of social change. The hero, Goetz is a romantic conservative, more than a bit out of touch with his times. . . . My version wasn't very good — too far from the original, yet not far enough to be a work in its own right. I have used it as a source for *Armstrong,* though, and a little for *Left-Handed Liberty.* So as a workshop piece it has served its purpose.

Arden, *Theatre at Work,* p.50

Throughout the play [Arden] is working within his own range and the cumulative impression is masterly, building up an elaborate network of court and peasant factions around the central group of knights in scenes that fall like hammer strokes. [Arden freely follows up] passages of all-out realism with abrupt transitions into irony: for instance, one blood-drenched battle scene (with pistols discharged at point-blank range into the stalls) leads on to an hilarious episode showing the defeated commander, surrounded by grotesquely caricatured staff officers, dictating a tactful memorandum to the emperor. The handling of court corruption (particularly a marvellous piece of boudoir rough and tumble between a defecting knight and an imperious courtesan) similarly combines realist immediacy with ironic detachment. There is not an inch of superfluous rhetoric in the text, and Mr. Arden skilfully differentiates between the idioms of the various social groups.

'Restoration of an Abandoned Classic',
The Times, 13 Nov. 1963

[On the television version] The historical realities and legends are unfamiliar to an English audience though the theme of chivalry in decay being given despairing life by individual heroism is universal enough. The romanticism, gloom, armour, and glory reminded me of Victor Hugo's *Les Burgraves.* . . . I remember from *Ironhand* atmosphere — the effect of sets and costumes — more clearly than character or plot.

Frederick Laws, 'Drama and Light Entertainment',
The Listener, 6 May 1965

Ars Longa, Vita Brevis

Written with Margaretta D'Arcy. Short play in seven scenes.
First London production: in Royal Shakespeare Company's
    Theatre of Cruelty season, LAMDA Th., 28 Jan. 1964 (dir.)
    Peter Brook).
Published: in *Eight Plays for Schools* (London: Cassell, 1964);
    and in *Encore*, No.48 (Mar.–Apr. 1964), p.13-20.

*An art teacher at a private school believes in rigidity and disci-
pline, so joins the Territorial Army. On an army exercise, he is
killed, accidentally-on-purpose, by the Headmaster, which frees
the teacher's wife to enjoy 'herself in fast cars with innumerable
young men'.*

Having accepted, rather casually, a commission to write a piece
for schoolchildren, I was at a complete loss until Margaretta
D'Arcy reminded me of a curious inquest, reported in *The Times,*
held on an art master shot in a wood while taking part in a
Territorial Army exercise. Peter Brook then asked me for a little
piece for his *Theatre of Cruelty* programme, and we thought we
would kill two birds with one stone. Miss D'Arcy had been doing
some improvised plays with children in Kirkbymoorside and also
in Dublin – or rather, they had improved their own plays with
her assistance, and she suggested that the peculiar directness
and the spontaneous development of 'classical' conventions which
we saw in their work would be a useful starting point. *Ars Longa*
is really more her play than mine – she decided what was to
happen in each scene, and I then wrote down a sort of stream-of-
consciousness dialogue to illustrate it. . . . I did not attempt to
polish or even revise this dialogue.

Arden, *Theatre at Work*, p.53

Armstrong's Last Goodnight

'An Exercise in Diplomacy' in three acts.

First production: Glasgow Citizens' Th., 5 May 1964 (dir. Denis Carey; with Iain Cuthbertson as Armstrong).

Revived: Chichester Festival Th., 6 July 1965, trans. to National Th., London, 12 Oct. 1965 (dir. John Dexter and William Gaskill; with Albert Finney as Armstrong and Robert Stephens as Lindsay).

First American production: Th. Co. of Boston, 1 Dec. 1966.

First French production: Compagnie du Théâtre de la Cité de Villeurbanne, 1966 (fully documented in *Les Voies de la création théâtrale,* 5, ed. Denis Bablet and Jean Jacquot, Paris: Ed. du Centre National de la Recherche Scientifique, 1977, p.281-343).

Published: London: Methuen, 1965; and in *Plays One.*

Armstrong is a semi-independent feudal chief on the Scottish border in the early sixteenth century. The Scottish King sends Lindsay to persuade Armstrong to end his raids into England, giving him titles. The King, to prove his good intentions, imprisons the overlord of Armstrong's rival, but Armstrong's own superior denies him the new titles. Armstrong, who has meanwhile seduced Lindsay's mistress, is so angry that he raids England again. When Lindsay next visits Armstrong, the latter is being visited by a Lutheran Evangelist. McGlass, Lindsay's secretary, criticizes the Evangelist for sanctifying Armstrong, and the Evangelist kills McGlass. Lindsay goes to Armstrong a third time, inviting him to hunt with the King. The King, who has been tutored by Lindsay, meets Armstrong disguised, reveals himself, and orders the immediate hanging of Armstrong.

With *Armstrong,* it began with a ballad which dramatized an account of his hanging [No.169, *The English and Scottish Popular Ballads,* ed. F.J. Child]. I thought I would like to write about him, but I couldn't yet find any meaning in the story. I was turning the idea over when I read Cruise O'Brien on Katanga [*To Katanga and Back,* 1962], and I began to see parallels to the Congo situation.

Arden, 'The Theatre of Bewilderment', p.7

The main point of the play will be the problem of achieving peace in a disorderly community, which is basically the moral problem posed by Conor Cruise O'Brien in his book on Katanga. Armstrong will be a character rather like some of these African politicians. There's a type of man at present in these new countries in Africa who seems to have this curious combination of practical ruthlessness with almost hysterical emotion, which you don't find in European politicians much these days but which certainly you did in the sixteenth century. I mean a man like Lumumba who was commonly represented in the western press as being almost a certifiable lunatic would have got on perfectly well with the people at the time of the Wars of the Roses. You know, they would have understood this bursting into tears in public speeches. I'm also faking up a political character based on Conor O'Brien of whom there is quite a good historical original — a man called David Lindsay, the author of the *Thrie Estates*; he was both a poet and a diplomat.

> 'Arden Talking about His Way of Writing Plays', p.19

Sixteenth-century literary Scots is not the same thing as Burns — it's a Latinate, rather pedantic language, and if one is going to introduce upper-class educated characters they'll have to speak it; it would be quite wrong to have them in nondescript modern English. It's a question of selecting enough Scots usages to give the language flavour, without writing deliberate pastiche.

> 'Arden Talking about His Way of Writing Plays', p.19

I find the whole sequence of events in the play so alarming and hateful (while at the same time so typical of political activity at any period) that I have — perhaps rashly — taken for granted a similar feeling among the audience. . . . My views on the Armstrong story are positive enough — Lindsay was wrong. But as to what he should have done to avoid self-destruction: there is a question that I cannot pretend to answer. . . . Lindsay's problem would not have arisen, at all, had he not subscribed to the belief in the necessity of government, and had he not undertaken to further this belief by serving the King. There is a basic contradiction between such service and the ideals of individual humanity that he expresses in my first act, and because he fails to detect this inconsistency, all his troubles come upon him.

> Arden, 'Letters', *Encore,* No.51 (Sept.-Oct. 1964), p.51-2

Arden is to me a writer a bit like Shakespeare in his approach, in that the writing not only has to convey the communication, the dialogue of characters speaking together, but also has to carry the sense of the social environment, and the texture of the people's lives; in addition it has to carry the writer's attitudes and his philosophies about the situation. All that has to be supported by language. Now what I think is marvellous about *Armstrong* is that Arden pulls this off.

William Gaskill, 'Producing Arden',
Encore, No.57 (Sept.-Oct. 1965), p.23

What the play offers is an image of violence and statecraft rather than an analysis. Arden's main interest is in narrative: see what happens when this kind of man confronts that type of man, and draw what conclusions you will. A chronicle play may not be the highest kind of drama, and arguably Arden is unduly absorbed in the picturesque possibilities of his subject, the opportunity to display the primary colours and barbarous com-plots of the ballad-world which he loves. If so, the price is worth paying, for it ensures that he respects the sheer *otherness* of the past, instead of regarding it merely as an adjunct to the present. . . . Two qualities raise Arden well above the level of competent reconstruction. The first (which is what makes him a true dramatist) is that his characters really engage and grapple with one another. Sir David Lindsay's rough reception at Armstrong's castle, for instance, with the courtier, his arms pinioned, gauging just how far he can ridicule the outlaw, just when to play on his vanity, is a beautifully taut contest for mastery. Arden's other basic strength is his feeling for language. . . . Arden knows . . . how to strike home with a sardonic phrase ('Ye are indeed cause for an itchy paragraph or twae in some paper of state'). He is particularly successful at catching a characteristically Scottish blend of bluntness and formality, the intimate and the pedantic. His characters talk like lawyers at one moment, peasants the next. . . . The play is too long, and there are some lumps in the porridge, notably the episodes of the distraught girl and the sensual evangelist. . . . The over-all effect, however, is one of spiky integrity.

John Gross, 'Rebels and Renegades',
Encounter, Oct. 1965, p.41-2

Arden's work throws up visual images very vividly. There is a clump-footed reel that looks like a Brueghel, an almost cinematic shot of a girl lugging the corpse of her untrue lover into the woods, a hanged body that turns like a salmon on a hook, a ring of soldiers with jagged black hair sitting in a Japanese-looking squat with one knee up and one on the ground. They are the sort of pictures that a child retains from narrative poetry read aloud, part of the world of ballad, like most of the other good things in the play: sweet love scenes and swift treacheries, a sense of tragedy that is cool and rather chaste.

Penelope Gilliatt, 'Adjusting the Focus of History',
The Observer, 11 July 1965

Left-Handed Liberty

'A play about Magna Carta' in three acts, commissioned by the City of London to mark the 750th anniversary of Magna Carta.

First London production: Mermaid Th., 14 June 1965 (dir. David Williams; with Patrick Wymark as King John).

First American production: Boston Th. Co., Jan. 1968.

Published: London: Methuen, 1965.

A dark stage, two pools of light. In one, a golden diagram of the Ptolemaic circles, emblems of order, government, and cohesion. In the other, Pandulph the papal legate, addressing to us a homily about the state of the world. He tells us, directly and calmly, that nothing has really happened since the Crucifixion, nothing can happen until the Second Coming. We are sucked into the time, the flavour and perspective of the thirteenth century, effortlessly. Arden puts us right inside the medieval world at one bold stroke.

Michael Kustow, *'Left-Handed Liberty'*,
Encore, No.56 (July-Aug. 1965), p.39

A queen snaps into view, sitting on a high throne, rigid with age and about to die, with ten feet of robes and furs pouring down to the floor like guttering wax; she mutters some incomprehensibly personal history and is removed suddenly backwards, throne and all. Liberated by his mother's death, a tub-shaped King John with a choleric sense of humour starts to swoop over the stage as though England were the chessboard in Alice.

Penelope Gilliatt, 'Plantagenets and Philistines',
The Observer, 20 June 1965

John negotiates Magna Carta with the barons, led by Fitzwalter and De Vesci. The Marshal and Archbishop enter, torn between duties to King, barons, country, and Church. The Charter is sealed, and John's recruiting of mercenaries and the garrisoning of the Tower discussed. The next scene, with dance, song and a dice-game, shows the barons with their whores; then the King whimsically dispenses justice. Six more scenes report the events of the Civil War, which resumed two months after the signing. Then John takes on a present-day existence, justifying and explaining himself, finally drowning in an episode using mime, verse, and prose summary.

I made radical changes to the dialogue, particularly of the last act, during the final stages of rehearsal, as may be discovered by any-one who is able to compare the prompt copy with the prematurely printed text. [In fact the prompt copy shows substantial deletions, but only Scene 7 of Act 3 is much changed, expanding the 1965 references.] . . . I did not accept the job until I had read some books, and then, although the story did not seem naturally to lend itself to dramatic form, I found myself sufficiently interested to carry on. . . . It is a bit of a chaos.

Arden, *Theatre at Work*, p.55, 52

Left-Handed Liberty is about the feudal system beginning to crumble but it *is* a system which was temporarily successful.

Arden, 'Questions of Expediency', p.15

Perhaps I view [John's] character and motives too favourably. It is difficult, however, to resist the rather weird charm of any of the Plantagenets when one comes to examine their personalities at close range.

Arden, 'Author's Notes', *Left-Handed Liberty*, p.xi

It is clotted with ideas, bereft of characters, full of stage pictures stamped out like shots in a film, and defiantly concerned with questions that would strike most contemporary dramatists as barren.

> Penelope Gilliatt, 'Plantagenets and Philistines',
> *The Observer,* 20 June 1965

An anatomy of liberty, the value of treaties, the irony of historical fact, these are the themes and they are cleverly discussed, but good themes though they are they prove top-heavy for this play, or rather for its author. John Arden the individual sinks under their weight, leaving great chunks of writing which might cheerfully belong to any one of half a dozen people – Anouilh, for instance, in *Becket* mood, or Osborne after *Luther,* or Brecht of course, or even Christopher Fry. The Arden of earlier days peeps through from time to time, in a couple of blistering images in the third act and in the ironic treatment of Pandulph throughout, but this is essentially an exercise, a history lesson well prepared and cunningly presented.

> Frank Cox, *'Left-Handed Liberty',*
> *Plays and Players,* Aug. 1965

There is not much blood in the writing. Intelligence is no substitute for imaginative energy; and apart from odd glints of wintry comedy and a couple of scenes which show off the King's peremptory tactics, the play resembles an elaborate piece of mechanism impressive in all respects except its failure to work.

> 'John Arden's Brechtian Look at Magna Carta',
> *The Times,* 16 June 1965

Friday's Hiding

Written with Margaretta D'Arcy. Short play, largely in mime: 'an experiment in the laconic'.
First production: Royal Lyceum Th., Edinburgh, 29 Mar. 1966.
Published: in *Soldier, Soldier, and Other Plays.*

A mean Scottish farmer is so reluctant to pay his two labourers that every Friday afternoon produces a serio-comic situation in which he hides while the men scheme to wheedle their money from him.

It is intended (beneath its farcical surface) to be an accurate representation of certain features of modern country life. . . . The play in sum is an ironic statement − *not* an affirmation − of the deep rootedness of conservative values.

Arden and D'Arcy, 'Authors' Notes',
Soldier, Soldier, and Other Plays, p.178-9

The Royal Pardon

'or, The Soldier who Became an Actor'. Written with Margaretta D'Arcy. Play for children in two acts.
First production: Beaford Arts Centre, Devon, 1 Sept. 1966 (dir. Arden and D'Arcy).
First London production: Arts Th., 20 Dec. 1967.
Published: London: Methuen, 1967.

In a 'legendary rather than historical' past, travelling troupes of actors receive a royal pardon and are summoned to compete before the king. One group, joined by a soldier back from a war, perform King Arthur *and win. They go on to France to perform at a royal wedding and to compete successfully against a French company, despite a comic Constable working against them.*

The play had its origin in a series of bedtime stories told to our own children (aged two to six): but we intended the dramatized version to be for a somewhat older age-group.

Arden and D'Arcy, 'Authors' Note', *The Royal Pardon*, p.7

Mixing echoes from *Henry V,* Hardy, and medieval St. George plays, [Arden] weaves a feeling of deeply English legend, simple but full-blooded.

Ronald Bryden, 'Writing for Children',
The Observer, 24 Dec. 1967

[The play] can be taken either as a straight tale about strolling actors, a variation on the illusion-reality theme, or a plea for popular drama against drama for the privileged few.

Irving Wardle, 'Give the Child a Chance',
The Times, 23 Dec. 1967

41

Harold Muggins Is a Martyr

Written with Margaretta D'Arcy and CAST [Cartoon
   Archetypical Slogan Theatre]. Play in two acts.
First London production: Unity Th., 14 June 1968 (dir. Roland
   Muldoon and others; with Arden and D'Arcy as Mr. and Mrs.
   Muggins). *Unpublished.*

*Muggins and his wife run a small, struggling cafe, dealing on the
side in pornography, prostitution, and stolen goods. Grumblegut,
a businessman, and Jasper, an accountant, take over the cafe,
which is renamed the Subliminal Experience. Muzak and fruit-
machines are added, customers fight, loyal employees leave, and
'the Organization' deducts protection money, so Mrs. Muggins
recruits a local gang to resist: the gang takes over and begins an
orgy. A battle follows: 'terrible mayhem; nobody left apparently
alive at the end of it except for the Muggins and Grumblegut'.*

One did feel a need to break away, at least temporarily, from the
conventional theatre. Yes, I have been trying for a long time to
find the right way of saying the things I want to say.... The plot
was worked out last year during a series of improvisations. The
cast had never worked with a script before. You might say it's
like *commedia dell'arte,* improvised round a set theme.... It's
really about how [Muggins] gets into his situation. The play
doesn't give a verdict on him, it's not a directly didactic play.
We're not saying 'look, the guilty man'; the verdict is implied.
                    'Interview: John Arden, at Work on a New Play,
                    Talks to John Peter', *Sunday Times,* 9 June 1968

Arden coming from Yorkshire was imbued with Messianic rage
about the thinness and feebleness of language in the media,
regarding this as theft of the working class's natural heritage....
We got a lot out of the Unity project: because we had done such
a variety of things in it, culminating in an improvised version of
the play for local kids on a Sunday afternoon as part of a big
party. Roland [Muldoon, the director,] dropped his lighting-plot
and tableaux, we dropped the written script, and the result was a
fast-moving, funny panto, with the actors influenced but not

enslaved by the rhythms of the original language.

> D'Arcy and Arden, quoted in Catherine Itzin, *Stages in the Revolution* (London: Eyre Methuen, 1980), p.344

Surely the stupidest play ever written by an intelligent writer. Hasty, inept, profoundly patronising, it's an embarrassing demonstration of how not to write down to the imaginary prejudices of an audience. . . . Arden has contrived a British equivalent of Brecht's *Arturo Ui.*

> Ronald Bryden, 'Romantic *Muggins*', *The Observer,* 16 June 1968

The political message is familiar. It amounts to a howl of laughter, occasionally anguished, against the plastic society and its echelons. . . . If *Muggins* simplifies issues, as good propaganda invariably has to, it never simplifies people, stylize them how it will. Even Muggins, though he falls for the blandishments of protection-racketeers, is not altogether detestable, but a silly man caught up by circumstances. . . . This sense of ambiguity underlines and leavens the political directness.

> Simon Trussler, 'A Refresher Course for the Purpose of Politics', *Tribune,* 21 June 1968

The True History of Squire Jonathan and His Unfortunate Treasure

Play in one act.
First London production: Ambiance Lunch-Hour Th. Club,
   17 June 1968 (dir. Ed Berman).
First New York production: Hamm and Clov Stage Company,
   AMDA Th., 21 Dec. 1974.
Published: in *Plays and Players,* Aug. 1968; and in *Two Autobiographical Plays.*

A room with a harp, a wooden chest, a brass horn which also serves as a telescope, a fire, and a stool. A low white wall suggesting battlements surrounds the room, with a toy drawbridge on one side. Outside is grass and a muddy pool. Jonathan squats by the fire; he has long lank red hair, faded velvet doublet and hose, and a key in his belt which, he says, unlocks his jewel chest. He yearns for 'a mountain of a white woman', for 'without such a woman all this treasure is worthless'; then such a woman arrives. Jonathan undresses her and adorns her with jewellery, but cannot unfasten her chastity belt. Then he finds she has a black tooth and suspects she has come to make him 'a laughing-stock'. She removes all the jewels except a belt, takes off her chastity belt, and jumps out of the window into a blanket held by 'the Dark Men'. Jonathan says: 'I am not yet defeated'. Arden's Preface explains that the play was prompted by his being in love with 'a large blonde beautiful Scot', who rejected him. 'By 1963, when I wrote the play, I no longer bore anybody any malice.'

As good a way of spending lunch-time as one can possibly think of: much more fun, in fact, than visiting the National Gallery and watching netball in Lincoln's Inn Fields combined.

Philip French, 'Laughing Stocks',
New Statesman, 28 June 1968

Its black charcoal-burners roaming in the forest round Square Jonathan's house recall *The Lord of the Rings*, but one feels that Mr. Arden must have intended more than a literary exercise. . . . It may be a parable of the ineffectualness of capitalism (since the lady eventually escapes); or a demonstration that it is possible to combine striptease with considerable elaboration of language.

Harold Hobson, 'Theatre and Drama',
Sunday Times, 15 July 1973

In spite of being billed as an erotic comedy, it was mordantly reminiscent of Ghelderode rather than of Aristophanes. . . . Whether the purport of [Jonathan's] impotence − in the wake of chastity unbelted − was so obvious as to be trite or so subtle as to escape me must remain unresolved.

Simon Trussler, 'Safety in Numbers', *Tribune*, 5 July 1968

The Hero Rises Up

Written with Margaretta D'Arcy. 'A Romantic Melodrama' in three acts.

First London production: by the Institute of Contemporary Arts, the Roundhouse, 6 Nov. 1968 (dir. Arden and D'Arcy; with Henry Woolf as Nelson).
Published: London: Methuen, 1969.

Nelson is considered as 'the last uncontested hero-figure of our own history'. Act I, set in Naples in 1799, shows Nelson restoring the monarchy and having the republican leader hanged, an action which brings about his sexual success with Lady Hamilton. Back in England in Act II, Nelson rejects his wife, and Lady Hamilton performs her 'attitudes' at a drunken party which ends in a burning of radical books. After destroying the Danish navy at Copenhagen in 1801, in Act III Nelson copes with irritating relatives, is killed while winning at Trafalgar, and finally ascends to heaven in a gilded chariot. accompanied by both his women, singing: 'The hero rises up to reach/His everlasting proud reward'.

The British public prefers to do without wars and to make love whenever it can. The top brass cannot do without wars and has nothing to do with love. Nelson belonged to both categories and I suppose that is why books are continually written about him and his campaigns and his life with the ladies. . . . He was all wounds and human weakness, [Lady Hamilton] was the eternal barmaid/tart/stripper-with-the-heart-of-gold, and between them they seem to have added up to all that was worth fighting for by the ordinary English in the England which they knew. . . . Yet their very humanity only helped to let people forget the essential *in*humanity of his treatment of Lady Nelson and indeed the essential inhumanity of the cause of the war itself. Liberty, Equality, Fraternity were the enemy. England, too, professed Liberty and did little enough to prove its claim. It should not be forgotten that in Naples Emma and Horatio have a fouler reputation than Napoleon ever had with us.

Arden, 'Human Horatio', *Sunday Times,* 9 Mar. 1969

The form is that of a ballad opera enacted by puppets. . . . Words are chanted rhythmically to old airs and shanties, mostly in a tuneless, unaccompanied *Sprechgesang,* and the actors only act like puppets, with jerky, stylized gestures, full face to the audience. . . . Many of the supporting actors wear half-masks in the style of the *commedia dell'arte*. The spirit of the enterprise — or so I fancied — was roughly that of the crude farces played on the balconies of the fairground booths of Paris at the time of Nelson.

Frank Marcus, 'Another Patch of Hair',
Sunday Telegraph, 10 Nov. 1968

The play seems merely a new variation of the often-quoted line of Brecht's Galileo: 'Happy is the land that needs no heroes'. But, unlike Brecht, Arden is not trying to discredit an historical idol as a squalid criminal. Like Kopit's Buffalo Bill, Nelson survives with no loss in heroic stature.

Irving Wardle, 'Search for National Heroes',
The Times, 9 Nov. 1968

It is a serious portrait and a serious argument: the real Nelson, the true hero whom the British still adore, was not the stiff-backed slave of duty who executed Carracciolo, but the fallible, contradictory human being who flouted authority, bent regulations to suit himself and loved a fat, pretty demimondaine better than his wife. It is a simplified picture, but not without truth.

Ronald Bryden, 'Emma, the Goddess from Merseyside',
Observer, Colour Magazine, 26 Oct. 1969

The Ballygombeen Bequest

Written with Margaretta D'Arcy. 'An Anglo-Irish Melodrama' in two acts.

First production: St. Joseph's and St. Mary's Colleges of Education Dramatic Societies, St. Mary's College, Falls Road, Belfast, 1 May 1972.

First professional production: by 7:84 Company, Edinburgh Festival, 21 Aug. 1972, followed by national tour, including Bush Theatre, London, 11 Sept. 1972.

Published: Scripts (New York), No.9 (Sept. 1972).

Publication and further productions of The Ballygombeen Bequest *in Britain were prevented by a libel suit, eventually settled out of court in 1977. Cuts, additions, and changed emphases occur in the rewritten version,* The Little Gray Home in the West, *details of which follow.*

The Little Gray Home in the West

Written with Margaretta D'Arcy. Play in two acts, rewritten
version of *The Ballygombeen Bequest* (see p.46, above).
First public reading: The Sugawn, Highbury, London, 1 May
1978.
First production: Drama Dept., Birmingham University, Jan.
1982.
Published: London: Pluto Press, 1982.

*Baker-Fortescue, an English businessman, inherits a chalet and
fifteen acres in Kilnasleeveen, which he rents to wealthy visitors.
The family of sick, drunken Seamus, ever-pregnant Teresa, and
their children have for generations occupied a tumbledown cottage
rent-free in exchange for caretaking at the chalet. When Seamus
dies, Baker-Fortescue prepares to evict, and Padraic, Teresa's son,
returns from England and plans to resist the eviction. Secret
agents from Dublin and from the British Ministry of Defence
arrive. Padraic goes into Northern Ireland, is suspected of IRA
membership, beaten up by British troops, and dies. Dead, he
incites a comic fight between Baker-Fortescue and the contractor
buying the site of the chalet.*

[Arden explains that the play began when D'Arcy and he heard
that an old woman, Mrs. Fahey, was to be evicted in Oughterard,
their home town.] D'Arcy went to see Mrs. Fahey to discuss the
progress of the eviction suit, and was shown a pile of legal docu-
ments detailing the whole relationship between cottager and
landlord. She borrowed them for a while and we studied them
together. There was clearly a play in it. We decided that we should
write it and use it as a weapon in the agitation. . . . If enough
feeling could be aroused, not only locally but nationally, then
perhaps the retired naval officer would agree to proceed no
further with his threatened eviction.

> Arden, 'What's Theatre For?', *Performance*
> (New York), I, 4 (Sept.-Oct. 1972), p.12

A stunning political drama as good as the best of Arden and (let
me stick my neck out) an equal to most of Brecht. . . . *The
Ballygombeen Bequest* is more than a play about Ireland; it

conjured up a nightmare image of capitalism, friendless, tottering, and ultimately without hope or help.

Michael Anderson, 'Edinburgh 72',
Plays and Players, Nov. 1972, p.51

The Island of the Mighty

Written with Margaretta D'Arcy. 'A play on a traditional British theme in three parts'.
First London production (substantially shortened): Royal Shakespeare Company at the Aldwych Th., 5 Dec. 1972 (dir. David Jones; des. Timothy O'Brien and Tazeena Firth; with Patrick Allen as Arthur, Richard Pasco as Medraut, and Estelle Kohler as Gwenhwyvar).
Published: London: Eyre Methuen, 1974; and in *Plays and Players,* Feb. and Mar. 1973.

Arden's 'Preface' explains the various literary influences on this play: reading Malory at school, which he linked with the north-west Yorkshire landscape, reading Robert Graves's The White Goddess *at university, and later* Crazy Sweeney, *Geoffrey of Monmouth, and the* Mabinogion. *These helped to shape plays first drafted in 1953 and 1955, with Merlin added in the later one, and subsequently a television trilogy commissioned by BBC2 and written in 1966-69, which was rejected. The final version, written in 1970-71, was influenced by D'Arcy's contributions, travel in India, conflict in Northern Ireland, and Indian folk-plays. A long and complicated play, it has 33 named characters, plus companions, other Chief Poets, monks, messengers, fighters, peasants, madmen and women, and soldiers' wives. The time is the early sixth century, with Britain divided amongst semi-independent princes, including Arthur, aged seventy. His Chief Poet, Merlin, explains 'in his lineage and language he is both Roman and Briton. By religion he is Christian, and his work is to defend civility and Christianity from one end of the Island to the other'. In Part I, 'Two Wild Young Noblemen', Arthur deals with such problems as an invasion from Germany in the north-east, a revolt by Pellam in the Wirral, and the Wild Cat Picts rising against his nephew in Galloway. Interwoven with Arthur's planning and fighting is the story of the noble twins, Balin and Balan. Balan becomes the Sacred King of the Picts for a year and a day, then he is forced to fight Balin and they kill each other. Part II, 'Oh the Cruel Winter', begins with a meeting of Chief Poets, after which Arthur impulsively marries Gwenhwyvar. She joins Medraut and they defeat Arthur at the battle of Camlann. Part III, 'A Handful of Watercress', shows Merlin, insane after Arthur's death, with old Morgan and later with a friendly Cowman's wife – then the Cowman kills him. Meanwhile Bedwyr, with Arthur's broken sword, is retreating, accompanied by the poet Aneurin.*

The Arthurian Cycle of Legends is sometimes known as the Matter of Britain: it is in fact our national myth. It may once have been told at length by some old-Welsh Homer – but, if so, his works have been lost. Like most similar cycles, it derives from a period of tribal migration and land-settlement, resulting from the disintegration of a comparatively orderly, if oppressive and effete, social system. The *Iliad* and *Odyssey* dealt with the mess left in the Aegean after the fall of the Minoan civilization: the Hindu *Ramayana* described the expansion of barbaric Aryan peoples into the decadence of South India and Ceylon: the *Red Branch Cycle* celebrated the energy of the Ulster Gaels, then newly arrived in Ireland. The Matter of Britain is the story of what happened after the Roman Imperial administration had been withdrawn from this island.

The Britons reverted to a tribalism, which, although politically inept and self-destructive, was accompanied by a strong sense of liberty and individual pride. The invading English (Anglo-Saxons) did appalling damage: but, after intermarriage with the Britons, and once they had learned a measure of the native poetic tradition, they proved in the long run to have absorbed as much as they destroyed. It was, of course, a *very* long run. It is not concluded yet, as can be seen by the number of Welsh patriots hauled before the courts for various militant assertions of their identity.

National myths of this sort present a picture of a way of life remarkably similar to that which exists today in the 'Third World' – by which I mean those parts of the globe that have been occupied and exploited by one or other of the great modern Empires. . . . The Third World of our own day will find its own Homers from among its own people. We have attempted no more than to indicate – from a rocking and sinking post-Imperial standpoint (for what else is the stage of a subsidized London

49

theatre in 1972?) — something of how the early history of Britain foreshadows twentieth-century turbulence. . . . 'Kynge Arthur is nat dede' — but he seems to have changed sides. The true voice of liberty is more likely to be heard today from the kind of men and women who have little part to play in the traditional tales: I mean the ones who did the work, who fed and housed the noble warriors, and equipped them for their fight.

> Arden, 'The Matter of Britain', *Flourish*
> (RSC newspaper), No.3 (1972-73)

It's about land hunger. At the time of Arthur people pushed west from Asia till some fell in the sea and came to England. And the play is about this, and about the ordinary people, who live daily lives through these massive upheavals, and how they are affected while playing no conscious part whatsoever in these violent changes in their lives and history.

> Arden, quoted by Pam Gems, 'The Island of the Ardens',
> *Plays and Players,* Jan. 1973, p.17-18

[The Ardens attended rehearsals, but two weeks before the opening] 'we both felt at the run-through that, among other things, the meaning of the play had been crucially shifted out of balance, producing an imperialistic effect alien to our original intentions' ('Distorted Meanings at the Aldwych', letter, *The Guardian,* 5 Dec. 1972). [They asked for a meeting with the whole cast. When this was refused, they announced themselves as on strike, as members of the Society of Irish Playwrights, and picketed the stage-door. Arden and D'Arcy describe the whole dispute in detail in 'Playwrights on Picket' in *To Present the Pretence.*]

[The designers of the RSC production felt that] it is a question of using the period as a device, to make the points of intention of the play clearer. The author uses the past as a metaphor, and it would be wrong to betray that by using the style of the present day in a mistaken attempt to emphasize the play's contemporary relevance. It may be that people will feel that our approach is a bit homespun, but it has been willingly entered into, so as to present as real people characters hitherto mythical. [Two 'points of intention' in the play preoccupied them.] First, that the society that Arden invokes is not so different from that of contemporary Third World countries, a society that allows the great majority of its members very little opportunity to make significant choices about how they live. Second, that the play deals in emotional attitudes, those of the 'cool-headed Roman' element in the play and the element that lives in the world of the Golden Bough, of matriarchal blood-rituals of death and fertility. These attitudes are poles apart.

A.C.H. S[mith], 'An Interview with Timothy O'Brien and Tazeena Firth' [the designers], *Flourish*, No.3 (1972-73)

The play is in no sense a museum piece. We're not saying 'This is what life was like in the sixth century AD'. . . . John and Margaretta . . . show how all these myths are man-made — that they serve the needs of a particular society. I think the play has got very strong links with *The Bacchae*. One of Arthur's mistakes is that he has consistently followed a male, rational, and military way of life in his later years. In his youth he was more anarchic, more wild, more open to the incestuous relationship with the daughter of Branwen. On this level the play seems to me a parable about what makes up a whole human being. The message of the play is very much like that of *The Bacchae*. Euripides' work treats the existence of instinctive forces in a very repressive male kingdom. A society which consists entirely of discipline and repression is an unhealthy society. Equally a society which is completely anarchic, wild, and without rules is an unhealthy society.

The Ardens have chosen a fascinating point of history for their themes. The society in the play is in a state of complete disintegration. The primitive, ritualistic world of the Picts is collapsing just as the arguably more sophisticated Roman side of Britain, represented by Arthur's court, is also facing disintegration. The play asks how men and women can live together at such a moment — what religious, moral, and political principles should they follow? It examines the situation on all levels — from the court of Arthur, the Maimed King, to the lives of the people who have opted out of society like the bandits and bondswomen who people the stage. . . .

John and Margaretta would argue that the women in the play are not given much of a chance. They are treated almost totally as sexual objects, or as bits of property to be moved around. Even a woman with the spirit and drive of a Gwenhwyvar can only make an impression on her society subversively. When it comes to an absolute showdown of power the men will take over at the end. I don't think John is merely saying that everything will be all right in that society if the feminine imaginative side is given more

51

control and licence. Gwenhwyvar is in many ways a very destructive person. Half the trouble is due to her failure to realize the political importance of what she is doing. Aneurin says of her at one point that she is just playing 'games in a garden'. She's still a little girl and does not understand what she is doing. . . .

One of the things which [Arden] explores in *The Island of the Mighty* is the role of the poet in a society. You've got different types of poet in the play. With the Pictish poet you've got a bard whose function in his community is still basically religious, he's the keeper of the rites, the observer of the rituals, a kind of High Priest. Then there's Taliesen, the poet who is most completely a political figure, a manipulator whose poetic instinct, one feels, has become totally formalized and practically extinct. Merlin, however, still thinks of himself as a genuine poet.

> 'David Jones Talks to *P&P* about his RSC Production of
> *The Island of the Mighty*', *Plays and Players,* Feb. 1973

The Island of the Mighty is written in a particularly clumsy way. There is the costume Arden who writes long explanatory speeches with lavish images, often in blank verse: and Ballyarden who delights in folksy wailing songs and slapstick.

> John Elsom, 'Supporting Stoke', *The Listener,* 14 Dec. 1972

The sheer proliferation of incident and information blurs any sense of emergent pattern or sense of the dimension of the play. It exists on an ampler scale than that to which the theatre is accustomed; and it develops more in terms of strings of events rather than in chains of cause and effect. The pattern makes itself felt more by internal echoes than by plot: as in the deadly duel between the two brothers Balin and Balan, caught on opposing sides, which forecasts the final division between Arthur and Medraut; or in the early attack on the sacred person of Merlin, forecasting his fatal last attack on the poet Taliesen. . . . The writing is eloquent, and graced with poetry, but again and again instead of lighting up the ancient world that slumbers somewhere in British consciousness, it seems simply odd.

> Irving Wardle, 'Too Many Trees for the Wood in this
> Forest of Arden', *The Times,* 7 Dec. 1972

The 'untidiness' reflects an energetic, questioning, stimulating mind, grappling with perhaps too many ideas; and the length seems inevitable, given the subject, which is nothing less than the decline of Britain from Roman stability into the disarray of the Dark Ages. Other playwrights might handle the relationship between a crumbling Arthur and a skittish, wicked Guinevere better than he: some might make more of the psychology of Balin, the impetuous warrior who ends by killing his own twin, Balan. But only the old, unrepentant Arden would have dared stride in, with his songs, rhyming couplets, gnarled, knotty prose, and glorious imagination, to chronicle an entire civilization and refashion as elaborate a myth as exists. He constantly astounds with his unfashionable boldness, as he hustles you from dukedom to dukedom. . . . Gradually, the moral tenor of these confrontations becomes clear, as it did in *Armstrong's Last Goodnight:* mind versus emotion, the cerebral male versus the intuitive female, order versus anarchy. . . . We don't only get an intellectually challenging (and marvellously spectacular) play, but also a curiously stirring one, as full of feeling for the oppressed and dispossessed as many a more ostentatiously 'committed' one.

Benedict Nightingale, 'The True Voice of Liberty',
New Statesman, 15 Dec. 1972

The Non-Stop Connolly Show

Written with Margaretta D'Arcy. 'A dramatic cycle of continuous struggle in six parts', of which the first two parts are one-act plays, the other four are each in three acts.

First production, lasting 26 hours: Liberty Hall, Dublin, 29-30 Mar. 1975 (dir. co-ordinated by Arden, D'Arcy, Jim Sheridan, and Robert Walker).

First London production: by Inter-Action at Almost Free Th., 17 May-1 June 1976 (in fourteen 'self-contained episodes — one per day, readings with music and songs', staged by Arden and D'Arcy, who also took part).

Published: London: Pluto Press, 1977-78 (five vols.).

The life of James Connolly, Irish socialist, unionist, and nationalist, provides the throughline of the six plays. Part I, 'Boyhood, 1868-89', shows his childhood in Scotland, getting and losing jobs, joining the army and going to Ireland. The opposition is represented by Grabitall and three Employers, who appear in all six plays. Connolly falls in love with Lillie and deserts to be with her. In Part II, 'Apprenticeship, 1889-96', he becomes Secretary of the Scottish Socialist Federation, makes a successful speech, loses an election and then his job. He is appointed organizer of the Dublin Socialist Club. In Part III, 'Professional, 1896-1903', he forms the Irish Socialist Republican Party, starts a paper, The Workers' Republic, *protests against the Boer War, lectures in America, and quarrels with the Party. Part IV, 'The New World, 1903-10', shows him back in America, holding various jobs during strikes, schemings, and betrayals involving people like Eugene Debs and such groups as the Socialist Labour Party, the International Workers of the World and the American Federation of Labour. Part V, 'The Great Lockout, 1910-14', presents Connolly as Union organizer in Belfast, founding the Irish Labour Party and becoming involved with women's issues; the second half traces the rise and fall of the Lockout in Dublin. Part VI, 'World War and the Rising, 1914-16', has a prologue concerning the legend of young King Conaire, bound by three prohibitions from druids, all of which he breaks. The structure is the progression among rival Irish movements towards the glory and defeat of the Easter Rising. Connolly struggles to decide whether to commit the Citizens' Army to the Rising, then Pearse inspires him to fight now. The doomed, heroic fight at the Post Office occupies the last act, then Connolly is executed – and resurrected, to say how the struggle had begun a world-wide and continuing movement.*

[We] decided that the one representative of Revolutionary International Socialism among the leaders of 1916 was undoubtedly the most important possible theme for an Irish play. If, as we discovered from our reading, [Connolly's] years in the USA were dogged by a perpetual inability to see eye-to-eye on politics with the American Socialist De Leon, then we would dramatize this feud . . . as though it were, say, the quarrel between the rulers of the world in *Antony and Cleopatra*. Marcus Antonius and Octavius Caesar fought for the mastery of the Empire with legions and massed galleys: De Leon and Connolly manipulated committee minutes and wrote letters to party journals. But the passions in both cases were equally huge – and so were the issues. . . .

Costumes were colourful and spectacular, not naturalistic. There were big, feathered head-dresses and purple wigs; all military persons wore elaborate scarlet or blue full-dress; Tory aristocrats had grotesque masks like birds of prey; members of Socialist parties wore white shirts, dark waist coats, workers' hats/caps and red neckerchiefs. Connolly alone consistently dressed and was made-up to look like the historical portraits. . . .

Realistic prose dialogue is alternated with formal iambic verse, and also with a brand of informal 'sprung-rhythm' verse with rhyme, assonance, and alliteration, carrying great variation in the length of line. This was intended as a vehicle for rapid vernacular speech. . . . There are inevitably certain areas of the script where detailed accuracy had to be sacrificed in favour of *essential* (or *emblematic*) *truth*. This is not an evasion of responsibility: it is rather an acceptance that the responsibility of the playwright is not the same as that of the historian. . . .

The main contribution of politico-historical theatre to contemporary public affairs . . . is not so much 'propagandist' as exploratory and educational. But it *is* propagandist in that it finally brings the authors, and consequently the audience, to some 'partisan' conclusion.

> Arden and D'Arcy, 'A Socialist Hero on the Stage', in
> *To Present the Pretence,* p.92-138

The dramaturgy of the show was influenced by traditional Irish forms. One well-known element in Celtic art is the intertwining of serpentine *motifs*. It is sometimes something of a puzzle to pick these out and follow them through. . . . There is indeed an 'ambiguous' villain in the *Non-Stop Connolly Cycle*. He has already appeared in Episode Two. It would spoil the game to reveal his identity: but we do offer this clue: he is *not* the man in the top-hat.

> D'Arcy, Arden, Gareth Williams, 'Interstates Left', letter,
> *The Guardian,* 22 May 1976

The most successful audience relationship I've had has either been with children or with the kind of audience that Margaretta D'Arcy and I were able to do when we did the Connolly plays in Dublin this year. We did them in the big trade union hall in Dublin, and presented them to an audience that had been arrived at by advertising almost entirely in the left-wing newspapers, trade union news sheets, and that kind of publicity. The result was that we actually had an audience for six full-length political plays, which was interested in the politics and regarded them as important to their daily life. This is an Elizabethan audience in fact.

[The plays] are written in an epic style that to some extent derives from Brecht, and to some extent from the lengthy dramas in the Indian theatre, which are in great part narrated. And of course the whole thing in the Indian theatre is costumed in the most highly stylized emblematic way, and we tried to do the same with the Connolly play. . . .

I find it very difficult to define precisely the type of artistic experience that this production was. It is something that combined elements of authoritarian direction from the author, plus a great deal of much looser, democratic joining in by all members of the cast. Everybody, for example, was expected to help in the donkey work of making the costumes and props, and to play some sort of musical instrument during the show. Everybody was somehow involved in all the departments of the theatre which are normally split up. . . .

> Arden, interviewed by Maria Kreisler, in
> 'Theatre of Argument, but a Theatre with a Point of View',
> *Elizabethan Trust News* (Sydney, Australia), No. 17
> (Dec. 1975), p.21-3

The audience sit bunched informally together on chairs in the centre of the Almost Free. The 'theatre' takes place in spaces and on platforms around them, against a backdrop of colourful cartoon murals, of gloating top-hatted British imperialism king-konging it over the wretched Irish workers. . . . Heavy-going historical drama? Definitely not. The show is shaped like a popular folk ballad.

> Catherine Itzin, 'Ardens' Achievement "Censored",'
> *Tribune,* 28 May 1976

I am notoriously resistant to that combination of didacticism, bad rhymes, folksiness, and revivalist bounce in which the authors, John Arden and Margaretta D'Arcy, now specialize; but there are, I agree, more indigestible ways of spending a lunchtime.

> Benedict Nightingale, 'Brain Cells', *New Statesman,*
> 28 May 1976

The first production of the play was lit with colour, masks, flashes of crazy cartoon wit; would one forget Queen Victoria's Jubilee procession, for instance? Or a very arch looking doll who resembled Pope Pius XII being carried across the stage earnestly pursued by a goonish W.B. Yeats and a Maud Gonne who was much his senior?...

The efforts to make Connolly and his relatives illustrious fall flat a lot of the time; there is a niggling veniality, a lack of drive, a supposition of audience awareness of contemporary political arguments. ... There is a wonderful grasp of dialect, of historical incident, of the odd revealing piece of poetry. The use of English is resonant, always clear and flowing. A few lines sum up a battle. A phrase evokes an era.

> Desmond Hogan, 'The Beating Down of the Wise',
> *New Statesman*, 11 April 1980

Like Shakespeare's history plays, *The Non-Stop Connolly Show* deals with public, not private, events. ... British drama for the last hundred years or so has dealt almost exclusively with private events. ... The play is an attempt to dramatize ideas. The style D'Arcy and Arden forge here is one in which the concreteness of truth is again and again demonstrated: the characters and the action constantly run up against the stubborn reality of apparently abstract notions, as for instance in Rosa Luxemburg's argument with Karl Krautsky, which is not merely an argument with the author's viewpoint clearly established, but has a concrete, dialectical relationship with actual events. ...

It is the image, not the surface reality, with which the play is concerned. All this goes back through that strand in twentieth-century theatre best represented by Meyerhold (whose disciple Eisenstein was) to the *commedia dell'arte*. ... *The Non-Stop Connolly Show* is a remarkable fusion of comedy and epic.

The play uses the repetition of set scenes for both comic and epic resonances. A meeting scene for instance may be presented with comedy, as in the meeting when the ISRP breaks up through inefficiency and drink; or with the intensity crucial to the development of the reform versus revolution theme as in the British TUC meeting addressed by the furious and desperate Jim Larkin. ...

The play is rather like a prism. We pick our way through the images of the show — Grabitall triumphant or with his back to the wall, smug or fearful or furious; Connolly fighting his way through the jungle of conflicting events, obsessive yet detached, quarrelsome with De Leon, pedantic with Larkin, new struggle coming out of defeat as surely as it comes out of victory. ...

The authors jerk us from one 'style' to another with alarming unexpectedness. Is it poetry or is it prose? Is it heightened language or ritualistic language, the language of public speakers or the language of everyday conversation? It is, at different times, all these. Different linguistic modes take us through different modes of perception. We see the action poetically, then conversationally, as statement then as evocation, and so on.

> Robert Leach, 'Connolly Reclaimed', *Platform* (London),
> No. 5 (Spring 1983), p.12-15.

Vandaleur's Folly

Written with Margaretta D'Arcy. 'An Anglo-Irish Melodrama' in two acts.

First production: by the 7:84 Company (England) at Nuffield Studio, Lancaster, Oct. 1978, subsequently toured to Belfast, Dublin Theatre Festival, Oxford, the Midlands, and South Wales (dir. by D'Arcy and Arden).

Published: London: Eyre Methuen, 1981.

'The Hazard of Experiment in an Irish Co-operative, Ralahine, 1831.' Vandaleur, an idealistic landowner in County Clare, believes his duty is 'the reform of the rural economy'. In Dublin he hears a speech by Robert Owen, preaching the co-operative dream. Vandaleur brings Craig from England to help him; poor tenant farmers become equal in the co-op and the first half ends with a good harvest. Problems follow. The High Sheriff watches the estate because its members include Micheal, wanted because earlier he killed a corrupt steward. The neighbouring absentee landowner, Baker-Fortescue, mistrusts its success and finally tricks Vandaleur into gambling: Vandaleur in the end bets the estate and loses. He disappears, and his wife Emily takes over and acts again as a traditional landlord. There is a complex sub-plot concerning illegal slave-trading and Micheal's love for Roxana, ending in Baker-Fortescue's suicide and Micheal and Roxana leaving for America, where he will help to form the Fenian Brotherhood. All the events are commented on by William Thompson, who is working to form a similar co-operative, and Anna Wheeler, his lover and a pioneer feminist.

In this play we tell the true story of how an agricultural co-operative commune was set up in the west of Ireland in 1831, how it succeeded beyond all possible expectation, and how just two years after its foundation it collapsed in a sudden and personal disaster just like the denouement of a melodrama of the same period. We also show how the ultimate failure of Ralahine (due to the original proprietor's retention of the legal ownership of the estate) reflected a particular flaw in Robert Owen's Utopian theory of Socialism. . . .

We do not pretend to have written a 'documentary play', although the main events in the story are all taken from E.T. Craig's eye-witness account of Ralahine, *An Irish Commune*. We have telescoped his narrative here and there, but in general have kept as close to the recorded facts as we could. We did however find it necessary to resort to unashamed invention in one principal area of the plot — the motivation for the catastrophe in the gambling-club. . . .

When we first embarked on the play we thought of it as a useful contribution to a better understanding of Anglo-Irish conflict: how reformist advances have continually been set back by aggressive reaction, driving the Irish people again and again to 'terrorist' methods: and how this process has so constantly been connived at and assisted by the blindness to their own inbred imperialism of even the most progressive British political and social groups. . . .

A plot, incidentally, of considerable complexity, which could only be justified by our need to interlink a number of political themes (Irish tenants, black slaves, co-operation *v* exploitation, co-operation *v* sectarian rivalry, revolution *v* reform, feminism, racialism, predatory sexuality, and so on, with all their contradictions) against a background of a society at a time of critical change.

Arden and D'Arcy, 'Preface', Vandaleur's Folly, p.v-xii

The material is fascinating and raises complex issues which deserve to be explored in the honest and direct way of David Hare's *Fanshen*. Instead, D'Arcy and Arden have staged their story as a Victorian melodrama, acted out in front of a model proscenium with painted backdrops. . . . It . . . has the unintentional effect of making the villain, a mad major and hell-raising, crowing and braying regency buck, the most charismatic character around, if not the most sympathetic. I can't go along with the extension of the Orange Order's oppression of the Catholic peasantry to the more complicated situation in Northern Ireland now. Presumably it's because they were aware of these stylistic deceptions that the playwrights needed to dress up their tale with over-contrived sub-plots involving the slave trade (which was already discredited) and a token bow to feminism.

Robin Thornber, *The Guardian,* Oct. 1978

Melodrama and Marxism have in common a certain polarization of positions with easily identifiable heroes and villains and good and evil ways of behaviour. The D'Arcy-Arden achievement in this play, subtitled 'An Anglo-Irish Melodrama', is to combine popular theatre techniques and a polemic dense with complexities, while avoiding the twin traps of becoming bogged down in a welter of discussion and trivializing the issues involved. A kind of Brechtian melodrama really, for there are shades of the Old Master behind such moments as the third-person narration in the scene where the commune is established, and the use of a pair of commentators on the action. . . .

Vandaleur's folly refers both to the agricultural co-operative commune he sets up and to his behaviour. . . . It is all set in a plot rich with the usual trappings of melodrama: action, secret assigna-tions, lovers, pathos, comic relief and sensation, which reaches its apotheosis in the fox-hunting scene where the prey is a young servant girl. And the whole is delivered in writing of quality which moves flexibly from plain prose to poetry, from stylization (such as the racy idiom given to the Major) to prose-poetry, from the atmospheric chill of the plaintive song ('It's an old song and a true song as cold as a bone, That I cannot stop singing till I come into my own') to the fiery emotions of the plea in the epilogue on behalf of the Republican cause.

Rosamund Judith Steen, *'Vandaleur's Folly',*
Gambit, No. 38 (1982), p.139-40

The Life of Man

Ninety-minute play for radio.
First broadcast: BBC, 16 Apr. 1956. *Unpublished.*

Set in 1856. A half-crazy sailor, Bones, relives for a girl his three-day voyage out of Liverpool on the sailing boat, The Life of Man. *The harsh captain, Anthract, cruelly punishes Jones, a Welsh shepherd forced to join the crew. On the third day, Sunday morning, Anthract orders the engines started, Jones comes on deck, the ship catches fire and sinks. Bones is believed to be the only survivor, but he believes Jones lived too. Arden comments that the influences on the play are the Homeric* Hymn to Dionysus, *a similar narrative in Book III of Ovid's* Metamorphoses, *and John Masefield's novels,* The Bird of Dawning *and* Live and Kicking Ned.

The crimp gang, the god, devil, or saint shanghaied aboard a cruel coffin-ship, tarts, witches, mermaids, a roaring Bible-hard captain, a bunch of fables and parables — perhaps one found more than had been written in — were all woven into an exhilarating radio play, radio of a quality we get very rarely these days. Where the story went by dialogue, the talk was taut and authentic; where it broke into verse, it flung itself into the magic winds. The elements of black superstition, a ship sailing on a Friday, whistling on deck and so on were only an evocative frame: the power came from the fine writing.
Francis Dillon, 'Fossicking',
The Listener, 22 July 1971

The Bagman

'The Impromptu of Muswell Hill.' Ninety-minute play for radio.
First broadcast: BBC, 27 Mar. 1970.
Published: in *Two Autobiographical Plays.*

The Narrator, Mr. Arden, sets out along Muswell Hill Broadway in search of an Evening Standard *and bumps into a gypsy woman who sells him an ex-army canvas bag. Alone on a dark moor, he is nearly eaten alive by four starving women, is rescued by the local Fs of L and O (Forces of Law and Order), and taken to town. As a stranger, he can only survive by providing entertainment for the jaded populace. Fortunately the contents of the bag prove a big attraction. At the word of command (in rhymed verse) a couple of dozen manikins obligingly act out the true side of their audience's natures: in the case of the mob, treachery and slaughter; in the case of the ruling class, ingenious sexual perversion. When the rebels, with whom the Narrator is forced to team up, ask the manikins to perform for them, they scuttle terrified back into their bag. At the end of the play, the Narrator's position is: 'All I can do is look at what I see'.*

'Dream-ballads', *Times Literary Supplement,*
31 Dec. 1971

It does reflect fairly enough the state of my mind in the spring of 1969. . . . The attitude of the central character at the end of the story is reprehensible, cowardly, and not to be imitated.

Arden, 'Author's Preface', *Two Autobiographical Plays,*
p.16-17

I was interpreted by some critics at the time as absolving the play-wright from having anything to do in society. I don't believe that, and I didn't believe it then. The play is a satire, a self-satire; if I were writing it now I would try to make that clearer.

Arden, quoted by Matthew Hoffman, 'Chuck Berry',
Sunday Times, 29 Jan. 1980, p.52

His play was a complete triumph — it was that mystical thing, pure radio. Fortunately, it was a shining piece of ingenuity as well.

Peter Porter, 'Arden's Dream', *New Statesman,*
10 Apr. 1970

Pearl

'A play about a play within the play'. Two-hour play for radio.
First broadcast: BBC, 3 July 1978.
Published (in a slightly expanded text): London: Eyre Methuen,
1979.

*It features an honest-to-God playwright in the 1630s, Tom
Backhouse, angered by the embroidered frivolity of the London
stage. And its eponymous heroine is a mysterious secret agent
who comes to England to try to organize an unholy alliance
between the King's various enemies: disaffected English Pro-
testants, aggrieved Irish Catholics, turbulent Scottish Presbyterians.
But* Pearl *goes on to show her collaborating with Backhouse on a
play that is intended to put steel into the anti-monarchist cause
and, at a stroke, reverse Puritan opposition to the theatre. In the
event, their play is treacherously rewritten and sumptuously
glamorized; its performance ends with Backhouse stabbed to
death, Pearl priapically humiliated and blinded, and any hope
of a Catholic-Protestant alliance irrevocably doomed.*

Michael Billington, 'Priceless *Pearl?*',
Radio Times, 15 July 1978

The sense of verbal performance flows on rich and deep, as though
the fear that he might be accused of echoing long-past schools of
writing had never entered his head. Blank verse, or speeches that
sound like blank verse, are liberally scattered; rhymed couplets
pop up all the time. The plot is complex, highly-seasoned with
the politics of then that sometimes seem the politics of now. . . .
A sombre play, lit by its language.

Paul Ferris, 'Arden's Succulent Plum',
The Observer, 16 July 1978

Pearl is built up of half-timbered Jacobean and extravagant theatre
fustian. Characters sonorously pronouncing 'I do most appre-
hensively misdoubt . . .'; courtesans speaking of 'the curvatures
of my white body'; someone saying of the local lord that 'he
has written to enkindle his whore' — such language doesn't
only send conviction flying, it brings out the fruity and the over-

ripe in actors' performances.

Peter Porter, 'Psychopomp', *New Statesman,* 7 July 1978

Serious matters — but handled in a way that I found puzzling at times. Not only did geniality keep breaking in when Mr. Arden was trying, like Oliver Edwards, to be a philosopher: the places where I expected him to be most effective, as in the scenes of collaboration between Pearl and Backhouse, were least convincing, and all the vitality, the passion, the splendid rhetoric went into the Irish grievance, the Puritan or Levelling prosecution, and Pearl's passion for the theatre. . . . What was so interesting about Arden's handling of his material was the deliberate avoidance of pattern. The neatly interlocking pieces of the puzzle, apparently designed towards a four-square completeness and catharsis, suddenly fell apart in blood and chaos, in random events with unlooked-for consequences.

Neil Hepburn, 'Magic Roundabouts', *The Listener,*
13 July 1978

Its base is not in fact, but in alternative history. . . . *Pearl* is also the title of a medieval poem, the subject of which is bereavement and the role of the beloved dead as intercessors. Like her name-sake, Arden's Pearl acts as a mediator. . . . The ending of the play is a radio *tour de force* — so much so, indeed, that it is hard to imagine any other medium presenting it with such power. Arden uses a kind of alienation effect with shattering force. . . . Suddenly Arden forces us to see that, if a Pearl should exist, she would do so at this level of blind beggar in the true historical context of the Civil War — and perhaps in the present civil war in Ireland too.

Frances Gray, 'The Nature of Radio Drama', *Radio Drama,* ed.
Peter Lewis (London: Longman, 1981), p.73-5

To Put it Frankly

Fifteen-minute play for radio.
First broadcast: BBC, 19 May 1979. *Unpublished.*

The Adventures of the Ingenious Gentleman Don Quixote de la Mancha

'by Miguel de Cervantes Saavedra, adapted for radio' in two parts of ninety minutes each.

First broadcast: 29 Sept. and 6 Oct. 1980. *Unpublished.*

The adaptation begins with Cervantes, a tax-collector of 55, unjustly imprisoned in La Mancha. The local priest tells him of an old man in the village who read many romances, which led him into curious adventures: this man becomes the model for Quixote.

What Cervantes is doing is experimenting with different levels of reality and exploring where fantasy merges with reality. He extends this in an interesting way. In the first part of the book Don Quixote goes off on his travels and his friends and relatives eventually get him back home by entering into his fantasy world and manipulating him through it. If Cervantes had finished it there it wouldn't have been anything like so interesting. But in Part Two it becomes much more complicated. At the end of Part One he leaves open the possibility of a sequel. Part One was so successful that many pirate editions were sold. It also inspired one of those flashy writers who can knock a book together in a fortnight to write a Part Two. So when Cervantes begins *his* Part Two he sets Don Quixote off into a world where those he meets have already read about him in Part One, where some of them have read the unofficial Part Two, and where others lay claim to acquaintance with a non-existent account written by a scurrilous Moor out to discredit Christian gentry. . . . The levels of reality become completely muddled. . . .

It's not like Dickens, where you can put it into dramatic speech simply by cutting three sentences in every four. If one tries to do that the whole rambling baroque style disappears into thin air. . . .

I have, for instance, only been able to sketch in one of the secondary themes of the book — the attitude of Spain to the Muslim world which, in view of our current preoccupation with Islam in general, racism, and the enforced movement of population, could well have been expanded. But the subject is there in the background. So too is Cervantes' implicit criticism of the world in which he lives: Don Quixote's assumption is that the society through which he moves is basically a fair one in which a few occasional wrongs need righting. But the author drops hints all the time that this is not the case: the people who mock Don Quixote's superstitious obsession with enchantment themselves accept the Inquisition and witch-hunting as the norm. . . .

Of course he's a joke. But not so much of a joke in his own time as he appears now. . . . The idea of a Christian gentleman fighting the heathen was not all that far from reality. . . . He was an anachronism, but only slightly . . . a ludicrous figure, but only as much as a man would be today who dressed up as a cowboy and went around trying to shoot people. Don Quixote, remember, aimed to kill.

Arden, quoted by Paul Vallely, 'Spanish Shadows',
Radio Times, 25 Sept. 1980

[Arden's] enormously rich historical imagination . . . supplies him with a winning basis. . . . He is able, with the greatest economy, to evoke the flavour of a period. . . . The result is vintage Arden: the poetry, of both the ordinary folk and the fantastical knight, is deep, dark, and powerful; the canvas is almost Shakespearian in the breadth of his portrait of Cervantes' society and its workings. The sense of theatre is electric and epic, in the Brechtian sense, in style; the humour and wit range from producing the urbane smile to the belly-laugh; and the themes of anarchy versus order and the relationship of the individual to society are fruitfully re-explored.

Paul Vallely, 'Popish Plot', *The Listener,* 9 Oct. 1980

Garland for a Hoar Head

Two-hour play for radio.
First broadcast: BBC, 25 Feb. 1982. *Unpublished.*

*A portrait of John Skelton, sixteenth-century poet and satirist. . . .
We meet Skelton first in his old age, taking refuge in the Countess
of Suffolk's house [at Sheriff Hutton, Yorkshire], a drunken,
lecherous, craven, weary, grumpy and grubby dotard, a 'crapulous
hedge-hog', snuffling and snoring. . . . In a series of dreams and
flashbacks, we are taken back into Skelton's earlier life, his taunt-
ing of the all-powerful Cardinal Wolsey, his flights to safety, his*

rows, and his struggles with the sins of the flesh.
> Val Arnold-Forster, 'The Power of Skelton's Pen',
> *The Guardian,* 27 Feb. 1982

[Skelton's poems provide a framework, or garland and Arden records that when he discovered Skelton at school] I realized I had turned up a poet whom I could not understand, in the ordinary sense of the word, but whose very incomprehensibility seemed crystal clear to my imagination. ... One was presented with an image of a poet all alone in the oppressive atmosphere of his sanctuary house, hiding within the shelter of a legally defined church precinct, relentlessly and ferociously turning his political grievances into surrealist verbal gold, stabbing at the paper with a pen like an engraver's tool. ... There is such a contrast through his work but the style is always recognizably Skelton ... [who] can move from majestic declamation to colloquial gutter-abuse or affectionate familiarity or to sudden sexual arousal in the space of half a line.
> Arden, quoted by Paul Vallely, 'Fiery Individualists',
> *The Listener,* 18 Feb. 1982

A dense and broodingly poetic play. Like all Arden's recent major pieces ... it examines the relationship between the writer and society. ... Surprisingly, for Arden, it is a contemplative play rather than one of action.
> D.A.N. Jones, *The Listener,* 18 Feb. 1982

The Old Man Sleeps Alone

'A legend for radio of the building of Durham Cathedral'. Sixty-six minute play for radio, commissioned for the BBC's sixtieth anniversary celebrations.
First broadcast: BBC, 22 Oct. 1982.
Published: in *Best Radio Plays of 1982* (London: Methuen, 1983).

Set in the twelfth century at the time of the transition from Norman to Gothic architecture, it is a glorious, earthy tale of spiritual dreams and earthly passions messily fractured yet seamlessly patched. It mischievously plaited together the future of a

church left half-built by the death of its French master-builder
with the fortunes of a blighted love affair when the builder's
daughter chooses as a husband, from two heir-apparent appren-
tices, the one she feels is most able to carry out her father's plans
– although the choice is not the one her body draws her to. . . .
This fabric . . . was woven on to a background of battle between
the bureaucracies of Church and masons. Mr. Arden seemed
particularly to relish his portrait of the secular-minded bishop . . .
who occasionally dips his wisdom into the petty skirmishes but
who is really far more interested in his collieries and the trouble-
some Scots.

Susie Cornfield, 'Earthly Passions', *Sunday Times,*
24 Oct. 1982

Very loosely, I've based a sort of comedy – a little fable – on
a true story. It's about medieval masons and their rivalries, and
how they use a so-called miracle to cover up their professional
incompetence.

Arden, *'The Old Man Sleeps Alone', Radio Times,*
2-8 Oct. 1982

Both a sprawling exotic representation of antiquity and a con-
voluted, unfocused allegory about how aesthetic ideas are realized.
'The Old Man Sleeps Alone', The Listener, 4 Aug. 1983

It throws up a number of fascinating lines of inquiry – into
ecclesiastical power and corruption; the mysterious and struggle-
torn world of the masonic guilds; and the links between aesthetic
form and developing technology – but it remains a resolutely
historical play. . . . It's a strangely disappointing work, intensely
private and just a little too archaeologically precise to really
engage the listener.

M.P., 'The Master Builders', *The Listener,* 14 Oct. 1982

The Manchester Enthusiasts

Written with Margaretta D'Arcy. Play for radio in two parts of
ninety minutes each.
First broadcast: BBC, 18 and 25 June 1984 (dir. Robert Cooper;
with Christian Rodska as Craig). *Unpublished.*

Returns to the subject of Vandaleur's Folly, *the commune formed
in Ralahine, County Clare, in 1831. This time the focus is on
Edward Craig, inventor, socialist and co-operative thinker, and
his wife, who came from Manchester to assist.*

'All our work together', says Margaretta D'Arcy, 'is based on the
theme of the struggle and the contradictions between reform and
revolution'. 'Ralahine shows that reform is not sufficient', adds
John Arden. . . . 'I don't think history repeats itself. There are
certain themes that re-emerge and people don't always find the
same solutions as the last time. But each time, the same patterns
are discernible.' . . .

'I think Vandaleur turned to the co-operative idea as a means
of surviving', says Arden. 'He was more intelligent than most but
he had been suffering from what all landlords suffered then —
vast numbers of people on the estate that he couldn't find em-
ployment for.' . . . 'When we wrote the stage play, we weren't
that interested in Craig. In fact, it was mainly a play about Irish
politics in the nineteenth century. In this radio play, we've
decided to approach it from Craig's point of view — Craig, the
Owenite co-operator, Chartist, Socialist, veteran of Peterloo.'

'He was an extraordinary person, Craig', says D'Arcy. 'We
found a great deal of material on him in the Co-operative Library
in Manchester, among it a medal and portrait remembering him as
a great inventor. But what interested us was the fact that, in this
period before the Great Famine in Ireland, before the Chartist
movement in Britain, the struggle of the Irish workers was inte-
grated into the English revolutionary movement. So the Craigs,
this young couple, in a way epitomized the best of English radical
thinking.' . . .

'The Owenite movement was a broad front — like CND today
or the movement that ousted Somoza in Nicaragua. The other
interesting thing about the co-operative at Ralahine was the equal
rights between men and women — very unusual at that time. And
the fact that the people had the vote at a time when no one had
the vote.

69

'But Ralahine collapsed because of the basic flaw that it was set up by the landlord. . . . It was a good reformist endeavour that fell down because they failed to make the revolutionary decision to demand the land from the landlord before it was too late.'

Howard Kinlay, 'A Vision of Equality', *Radio Times*,
16-22 June 1984

c: Television Plays

Soldier, Soldier

'A Comic Song for Television.'
First transmitted: BBC, 16 Feb. 1960 (dir. Stuart Burge; with Andrew Keir as the Soldier and Margaretta D'Arcy as Mary).
Published: in Soldier, Soldier, and Other Plays.

An unnamed Scottish private in a Northern town learns that the son of a local family joined his regiment, and that they have had no news of him for a long time. He goes to the family, pretends to be a friend of the son, moves in for a few days, seduces the daughter-in-law, and gets money. Before leaving town, he freely admits lying.

In *Soldier, Soldier* the experiment was to try to see if verse was a possibility on the small screen. . . . Such success as it had was due to its comic or satiric qualities, to its use of music, to the talents of the cast, and to the raucous vitality of Stuart Burge's production. . . . In so far as the verse of the play is colloquial and humorous, it is satisfactory; but where I allowed myself to fall into a more lyrical mood, it failed to work.

Arden, 'Preface', *Soldier, Soldier, and Other Plays*,
p.9-10

The soldier is an archetypal creation, burst out of context and striding about the world alone. He asserts the principle of freebooting arrogance with an inexhaustible vitality and total lack of shame equivalent to that of

Don Juan. His only language is the military, reworked by Mr. Arden into a poetic amalgam of parade-ground formality and barrack-room *argot*. ... The inhabitants in their match-box houses, subsisting on a vile diet of mild beer, chips, and yellow cake, are creatures of a sombre vision of society. ... The dwarfish figures, with their drooping moustaches and shapeless clothes, stand out grotesquely like Brueghel's misshapen peasants.

Irving Wardle, 'Jungle of Arden', *The Listener,* 25 Feb. 1960

Wet Fish

'A Professional Reminiscence for Television.'
First transmitted: 3 Sept. 1961.
Published: in *Soldier, Soldier, and Other Plays.*

A busy Yorkshire architect undertakes the reconstruction of a small fish shop. The actual work is left to the inexperienced young Ruth. The builder takes advantage of her, problems mount, and her colleague Krank (of The Waters of Babylon) *secretly buys the properties adjoining the fish shop.*

Wet Fish was an attempt to present on the screen a fictional version of one of my experiences during the two years I spent as an inefficient assistant in an architect's office. I wrote the play deliberately in a flat and naturalistic manner — having learnt something from *Soldier, Soldier* — in the hope that it would prove possible to use the documentary potential of the television medium to give greater vividness to my main theme — which is, of course, the physical progress of an ill-starred building contract. ... It worked quite well as a straight situation comedy.

Arden, 'Preface', *Soldier, Soldier and Other Plays,* p.10-11

Wet Fish was a beautifully constructed symbol of the rotting structure of English social life. ... The northern types and dialogue were entirely real. But even Mr. Arden's realism can go on too long. Working-class speech is not enough in itself to keep a play in motion.

Angus Wilson, 'Long-Distance Perspective', *The Observer,* 10 Sept. 1961

The themes of shoddiness in building and corruption in local government deserve dramatic treatment, and Mr. Arden's 'speculative' architect's office made a convincing storm centre for it. I liked the atmosphere of low endeavour, frustration, and sour joking among the well-intentioned and down-trodden juniors who did the work.

Frederick Laws, 'Fashion Leaves Mayfair', *The Listener*, 21 Sept. 1961

a : Fiction

Silence among the Weapons
Novel. *Published:* London: Methuen, 1982.

---

*Deals with the mysterious and violent contortions which
led up to the disintegration of the Roman Republic in
the first century BC. The leading characters are Marius,
Sulla, Cinna, Drusus, and Mithridates Eupator, except
that they rarely emerge as such: they exist only as they
affect the destiny of a limping Greek theatrical agent
called Ivory who, at the outset of the story, is in a nice
way of business in Ephesus, but who is suborned by his
tricky mistress Irene into becoming an agent of a more
varied kind. Ivory's fortunes, or rather misfortunes, in
both capacities, lead him to brood, edgily and elliptically,
on the contingencies of daily life in a politically corrupt
society as he is driven on his peripatetic way into Italy,
to witness the butcheries of the Social War, onto a pirate
ship off the coasts of Crete and Cilicia, and finally to a
reputed exile in Milan. Enmeshed in its snarling paranoia,
the brutalities of its language and of its attitudes, the
overwhelming solipsism of its narrative, are some excellent
vignettes – of stage performances and private entertain-
ments, of rituals in the Temple of Venus – which convey
the spirit of the times rather more vividly than the
march of events.*
  Anita Brookner, 'Passion', *London Review of Books,*
                                          7-20 Oct. 1982

I'd been fascinated by Caius Marius ever since I read his
life in the Penguin Plutarch. . . . One night in the pub [in
Scotland in 1979] I was talking to an archaeologist
about what went on in the Roman theatres and we discovered that neither of us had the least idea; and no one
else had either. . . . By chance, I had a book out of the
library on the wars between Marius and Sulla and the
fact that the Greek states in the Eastern Mediterranean
were being taken over by the Romans. So I thought it

would be fun to write a novel about the changeover in my own profession from the Greek theatre to Roman entertainment. . . .

I was much more struck by a general similarity between then and now: between a central urban power being opposed by the people outside it and between events, say, in Chile and El Salvador. It's also a book about complex, shifting alliances. . . .

Graves deals with all the big people of the period, whereas I'm writing about fictional people who live at the lower end of society and only see bits of the power figures round corners. Actually the book I had at the back of my mind was a historical novel by John Masefield, *Basilissa*, about the Empress Theodora who was on the stage before she became a Byzantine Empress. Masefield wrote in a clear, precise language and saw people as people and not as figures in a historical book.

Arden, quoted by Michael Billington,
'The Drama Takes a Novel Turn', The Guardian, 26. Aug. 1982

Arden has often, in the theatre, gone back to history to find ways of making us look again at what is happening in our own time. . . . In this novel, he's clearly drawing parallels with the barbarity of our own civilization and, specifically, with events in Ireland. A section set in an Italian town called the Walls of Love describes the violence that erupts, following the scourging to death of a local freeman by the highway police, who are then supported by soldiers from the city. What makes Arden's plays so remarkable, though, is the fact that they're not simple schematic allegories. Their dramatic language is so rich that they create a concrete, detailed world of their own. . . . Arden creates such a world in this novel.

Albert Hunt, 'Cervantes' Trade', New Society, 2 Sept. 1982

b: Short Stories

'The Fork in the Head'
Published: in *Visitors Book*. Swords, Co. Dublin: Poolbeg, 1979, p.33-44

c: Poems

Children of Albion, ed. Michael Horowitz. Harmondsworth: Penguin, 1969, p.14-20
Four poems.

The Test of 'Vital Theatre' (1959)

Apart from the pantomime and music hall it is quite a long time since the mass of English people could find anything in the theatre.... Perhaps the last that did so was the Victorian penny-gaff melodrama, which may have been gutsy and vital, but was also pretty debased. What it was debased *from,* however, is a different matter, and one which should give us thought. I mean the Elizabethan/Jacobean Theatre, which held (almost) all classes together in the same audience. And the reason was not particularly Shakespeare, nor Ben Jonson, nor any of the other individual writers: but the still extraordinarily powerful popular tradition which informed that theatre as a whole. It was a tradition which can be traced back in a straight line through the medieval moralities and buffooneries, through the village mummers' plays with their strong fertility symbolism, to the popular Mimes of the Roman period and then right back to Aristophanes and beyond.

According to this tradition, tragedy and comedy were only two sides of the same medal: two not very dissimilar aspects of the continuous cycle of birth, creation, death, and rebirth — which is the only Poetic Theme, and by and large is the one thing which will hold the minds of an audience for that essential two-three hours *after* the fall of the curtain — the real test of Vital Theatre. Social problems of 1959 (or 1600, or 400 BC) are but a single part of the total pattern, and must illustrate it indeed; but in such a way as will at least *imply* the existence of all the other parts.

The true tradition is still with us, but it is buried deep down under several hundred years of puritanical falsification: the sad remains of it are traced by Richard Hoggart in *The Uses of Literacy.* But they are embers that are still susceptible of being blown into flame. Vital Theatre consists of plays which must be organic events — to get hold of their audiences by laughter, by pain, by music, dancing, poetry, visual excitement, rhythm: and occupy not merely the minds of the people ('Just like life, isn't it? What an interesting experience'), but their stomachs and their loins as well....

People must be able to laugh, not only at other people, but at themselves, and at the things that hurt them. The social purpose of the theatre is to bring men together in a kind of secular Eucharist, so that they can leave the building feeling that they *are* a society, not just a collection of odds and sods who have been coincidentally killing time for a couple of hours on a wet evening. It won't be easy to achieve this. It may not even be possible any more. But unless the dramatists can sit down quietly and take a long serious look back at the true origins and traditional subject-matter of the stage, they will have no hope at all.

'Correspondence', *Encore,* May-June 1959, p.41-3

Telling a True Tale (1960)

To use the material of the contemporary world and present it on the public stage is the commonly accepted purpose of play-wrights, and there are several ways in which this can be done. Autobiography treated in the documentary style (Wesker). Individual strains and collisions seen from a strongly personal standpoint and inflamed like a savage boil (Osborne). The slant-indicular observation of unconsidered speech and casual action used to illuminate loneliness and lack of communication (Pinter). Tough analysis of a social disease (Ibsen/Arthur Miller). And so on. What I am deeply concerned with is the problem of translating the concrete life of today into terms of poetry that shall at the one time both illustrate that life and set it within the historical and legendary tradition of our culture. . . .

The bedrock of English poetry is the ballad. . . . In the ballads the colours are primary. Black is for death, and for the coalmines. Red is for murder, and for the soldier's coat the collier puts on to escape from his black. Blue is for the sky and for the sea that parts true love. Green fields are speckled with bright flowers. The seasons are clearly defined. White winter, green spring, golden summer, red autumn. . . . What does this mean in terms of the theatre? To start with – costumes, movements, verbal patterns, music, must all be strong, and hard at the edges. If verse is used in the dialogue, it must be nakedly verse as opposed to the surrounding prose. . . .

Social criticism . . . tends in the theatre to be dangerously ephemeral and therefore disappointing after the fall of the curtain. But if it is expressed within the framework of the traditional poetic truths it can have a weight and an impact derived from something more than contemporary documentary facility.

'Telling a True Tale', reprinted in *The Encore Reader,*
ed. Charles Marowitz *et al.* (London: Methuen, 1965) p.125-9

A Plea for a Poetic Drama (1960)

The artificiality of the stage is one of its most important qualities. . . . People must want to come to the theatre *because* of the artificiality, not despite it: and if enough plays are presented that make a point of this quality, the harm done by too long an acceptance of the similarity between TV and theatre will in time be mended. . . . I am pleading for the revival of the Poetic Drama, no less. . . . There was such a revival hailed a few years ago, when Eliot, Duncan, Fry and others were thought to be the spearhead of the great movement. . . .

The real reason [for its failure to develop] was a basic misconception as to the true use of poetry in the theatre. Far too much effort was extended in trying to prove that it is possible to adapt the common conversational speech of today into a workable blank-verse line. Well, it *is* possible: we know that now. But somewhere in the process the essential blood and guts of dramatic poetry was forgotten. . . .

There are today certain trends in favour of a genuine theatrical poetry. Brendan Behan knows what is wanted, so does Ann Jellicoe. . . . It is not necessary for dramatists to write in verse — and if they do, there is no reason for them to involve themselves in Eliot's laborious theories of sprung rhythm and so forth — ordinary verse that rhymes and uses an iambic beat or a ballad stanza will do just as well. The vital point is that they must bring to their writing a sense of the theatre as a place where plays are made out of the details of ordinary life indeed: but where these details are treated as the stone in a quarry or the clay in a brick-field is treated by the builder of a tower.

'The Reps. and New Plays — a Writer's Viewpoint',
New Theatre Magazine (Bristol), I, 2 (January 1960) p.23-6

A 'Thoroughly Romantic View of Theatre' (1960)

I was brought up to take a thoroughly romantic view of the drama. . . . When I was thirteen, I was taken with others of the senior class to a production of *Hamlet*. . . . I found it hard to understand why modern plays needed to be written at all. . . . I imagined the commonest costume of the actor to be that of a past period, and the usual business of the scene designer to be the reproduction of Gothic Castles or Roman Temples. When I looked at books about theatre practice, I would pass over (as trivial and of ephemeral interest only) any photographs of plays in contemporary costume, and I would give all my attention to the illustrations and chapters that dealt with revivals of the classics or modern period pieces.

[In 1949, Arden saw Lindsay's *The Three Estates* at the Edinburgh Festival.] About the same time, I read an article on Brecht in the *New Statesman*. Although the author seemed to think he was describing something very novel and revolutionary, I immediately recognized what he was talking about. I did not know much about Brecht's theories then: I suspected, as I still do suspect, that he had few that had not been held intuitively by the Elizabethans. His revolution was to be able to put them into practice in his own theatre. . . . Such new plays as I saw depressed me very much. . . .

Many dramatists can work much more easily and happily if they have some reasonable expectation of a playhouse for their plays. . . . and if they are able to meet writers, producers, and actors fairly regularly in and about the normal working day, to discuss work, watch rehearsals, take a drink, and so on. . . . If the playhouse continues to exist, and if I can manage to write the plays I think ought to be written, and if the management will continue to put them on, then eventually the public will come to like them. It is an act of faith: just as is my adherence to that kind of drama which we may loosely call 'romantic' or 'poetic' or 'epic', and which I believe has had and will always have a more permanent basic appeal than any other, in spite of temporary shifts in fashion, because it is founded upon a wider and more inclusive view of life.

> 'A Thoroughly Romantic View', *London Magazine*,
> **VII**, 7 (July 1960), p.11-15

Writing for Television (1961)

Even the most carefully naturalistic production of the tightest slice-of-life play never manages to persuade the audiences that they are watching anything other than actors and constructed scenery – and why should it? The pleasure is in marvelling how well it has been done, in enjoying a superb display of theatrecraft: not in submitting to an illusion. . . . The *cinema* can produce a genuine illusion . . . TV lacks the godlike resources of the cinema. . . . The degree of naturalism is paradoxically increased rather than diminished. Instead of thinking, 'What a fine performance by Wilfrid Lawson' (as we should be if he were acting the same character on the stage or in a film), we tend to think, perhaps, 'How remarkably like that Birmingham dustman who was interviewed last night after finding ten thousand pounds in a dustbin'. . . . The dialogue of plays, of necessity, becomes more and more like tape-recordings taken in somebody's house. Hence the success of Pinter as a TV writer some time before the theatre world proper woke up to him at all. . . .

How much language can TV take? In general, not as much as the theatre. . . . There is a very useful purpose in the TV. There are always plays and bits of plays which one would like to write, but which seem too delicate or too unresolved for the stage. These may be themes that need another year or two to reach full fruition: but in the meantime, the TV can contain them, and their slightness will be an advantage. I mean, of course, slightness in *physique* — not in truth. . . . I myself wrote *Soldier, Soldier* for TV: and the following year I found that I was able to enlarge its themes to the length of *Serjeant Musgrave's Dance.*

'Delusions of Grandeur', *Twentieth Century,*
Feb. 1961, p.200-06

Verse in the Theatre (1961)

[Verse] is very much more packed and concentrated than prose. Thus, if the play is of a constant level from beginning to end, it is going to be practically impossible for an average audience to understand it at one sitting. If the play is not so packed, then the passages which are weak might just as well be written in prose. The Elizabethans used verse all the way through, but in the later plays of Shakespeare there is a tendency more and more towards prose. I think that they were aware that verse becomes hypnotic. When a character in Shakespeare's plays breaks into prose a new dimension is opened in the play. For instance, in *Henry V* there is the King's rhetoric which is in verse and being rhetoric is not really very good poetry; its subsidiary meanings are those of glory, gold, silver, sword, blood, and so on, and there is a slight phoniness about it, I take leave to suggest. Then there comes a prose speech in the middle of a play that says what it means, clearly, coldly, and precisely. When one of the soldiers says to the King: 'I am afeard there are few die well that die in a battle', having described all the legs and arms cut off in a battle, the use of words is economical and fulfils the best tradition of the best prose. Whenever I have seen the play, that part, if well-acted, has stood out from the verse, and I have a feeling that that is really the wrong way round — that nowadays we should be more concerned in writing verse passages that stand out from the prose, because since Ibsen modern drama has of necessity become associated with a realist depiction of contemporary life. The Elizabethans did this sometimes but nearly always they set their plays in foreign countries and distant periods. Nowadays this is done less and less in really good plays, and the use of prose to reflect and describe the everyday currency of ordinary speech has become more and more accepted in the theatre.

Our modern dramatist, like Pinter, uses the vernacular dialogue to a degree of elaboration and repetition so that it becomes like poetry, because, although it is not metrical, it employs poetic and rhetorical devices. In *The Caretaker* there is a man who is continually anxious to get down to Sidcup; he brings this in all the time, so that it becomes like a poetic theme. The prose there is beginning to work out of prose into poetry, and one feels that there is a desire to use straightforward prose to say things that prose does not normally say.

[Robert Graves] points to the Celtic tradition of epic writing, in which the bard would tell the story in improvised prose, with, interspersed in the story, certain passages of emotional tension which were composed in verse and which were verbatim and invariable. So there is always a loose story woven around certain definite poems, and I think that this is not a bad technique for us to bear in mind. I used this in *Serjeant Musgrave's Dance,* in the scene where the soldiers are on their way to the pub and the bargee says they are coming. Annie is asked what she thinks about soldiers and she speaks in quite regular ballad stanzas for sixteen lines. I could have written that in prose but I think to have done so would have involved a much more personal approach to the subject — one would have been more closely conscious of Annie's particular relationship with soldiers. When she speaks in verse, however, it gives an oracular pronouncement; it is Annie speaking from her own experiences but it is also a generalized comment on soldiers, which contrasts quite nicely in the play with a similar passage in the same scene when Mrs. Hitchcock is asked what she remembers about Billy Hicks. There she talks in prose, and gives a completely definitive portrait of Billy Hicks the man, without much external association. The audience's attention is there fixed on a concrete object, whereas in the other passage they are fixed on a general one. . . .

The transition between verse and prose is difficult. I personally do not worry too much about making it. . . . There is no reason, it seems to me, why the transition should be made at all, why the actor should not just come forward and say his verse bit, with everybody else talking prose. . . . It is asking the director to find a new style, just as it is asking me to do so. . . .

If we are going to say anything in our plays over and above the surface meaning of the words, we can and must do it in verse. . . .

I cannot too strongly warn people against believing that poetry began with Ezra Pound. Although poets should and must experiment as much as they like, if they do not keep at least one finger on the railway lines of strict verse form, they will end up by not writing poetry at all. . . .

People have told me, both in the columns of the newspapers and to my face, that they have not understood one or other of my plays — *Serjeant Musgrave's Dance* or *The Happy Haven,* for instance. I am sorry about this; it is not my wish. It is due to my disagreeably complicated temperament that will mess up what I want to be clear.

'Verse in the Theatre',
New Theatre Magazine (Bristol), **II**, 3 (Apr. 1961), p.12-17;
reprinted in *English Dramatic Theories: Twentieth Century,*
ed. Paul Goetsch (Tubingen: Max Niemeyer, 1972), p.111-7

The Matter with Britain (1961)

There is a great deal that is the matter with Britain. I do not think it is the business of dramatists to spend all their time putting it right. But if they bring to their work of the observation and the interpretation of life a proper moral concern and a constant hatred of injustice and meanness . . . they can be of permanent value in keeping the public mind aware of the standards of public life that wealth and comfort can easily obscure. . . .

There is no longer a vigorous peasant speech in the larger part of the country. Sixty years ago, Synge in Ireland, Masefield in Gloucestershire, Brighouse in Lancashire, and several others, were all trying to make a poetry, humorous or serious, out of regional dialects. This is not really possible any longer. . . . Nevertheless there is still enough variety and guts in popular vernacular for a dramatist to make something out of, when the tongues of the well-dressed would slip and slide over perfectly-enunciated syllables and convey neither meaning nor emotion. . . . Parliament is more or less without significant voice. If the drama is not to find itself in the same situation, it has to go out into the hedges and ditches like the man in the parable in search of the lame, halt, and blind.

'Some Thoughts upon Left-wing Drama',
International Theatre Annual, 5, ed. Harold Hobson
(London: Calder, 1961), p.187-96, 201-03

Aspects of Characterization (1961)

I have grave objections to being presented with a character on the stage whom you know to be the author's mouthpiece. It can work. Obviously in Shaw's play you know you are going to sympathize with Joan. But in a play in which the characters are complete fiction and you don't know beforehand what the story is, I don't see why we should always be given this cosy point of reference. It can produce awful sentimentality, particularly if the play handles any sort of social or personal problem.

How do you set about writing a play?

Granted an idea, which may take three or four months to germinate in my mind, I then sit down and write, not a full synopsis, but some very detailed notes. I find I can't satisfactorily write a synopsis for a play to a point much beyond the middle of act two. After that I have to leave it to the characters, as it were, to develop their own action in the last act. . . . I try to get the main lines of the personality down on paper in dialogue in the first two or three scenes, and find a rhythm for the character's speech. To my mind one of the most important aspects of character is speech rhythm. I like to give a character a particular turn of phrase which in life, of course, is always happening — people often use the same two or three little catch phrases — and all this helps to build up a picture. By the end of scene three, you may suddenly find that this character couldn't possibly do what you have laid out for him in scene four. The character now exists as a person, and you must rewrite the action round him rather than adjust him to fit the action.

Interview in *Theatre at Work*, p.43, 48-9

The Present and the Past (1963)

Plays should use speech in the same way that a poet uses individual images. One has to *form* language in the theatre rather than just *report* it. There has to be a tension and rhythm in the language; even if one is using ordinary colloquial speech it has to be carefully worked over so that it comes to have a dramatic rhythm which is not quite that of ordinary talk. . . . One should use verse in the same way that a costume designer will use a bit of gold here and there. . . .

One has to be careful about this business of heroes nowadays, because you find yourself getting back to the preconceptions of Elizabethan tragedy which don't belong to our society at all; there's no room for the titanic figure. Whether you accept Marxist theories or not you can't help being influenced by them: society with a capital S is a more interesting thing than the individual, and if you do produce a figure that stands out of the play it's almost by accident. . . .

The contemporary world and the past world fuse together — for instance, you can't write about modern politics without thinking in terms of history. After all, history does repeat itself in a general sense. . . . The moral questions involved are absolutes that apply to almost any period, and one is given a much easier field for drama by finding a period which is over and done with in order to set these problems out.

> Interview with Irving Wardle, 'Arden Talking about His Way of Writing Plays', *The Observer*, 30 June 1963

On Passion and Points-of-View (1963)

I think that one of the prime functions of the theatre has, since the earliest time, Aristophanes and beyond, been to inflame people's lusts, in something like the same sort of way as the tragedies produced a purgation of the spirit. . . . It should be possible to go to a theatre to see a show that provides you with a sexual excitement, and at the same time doesn't leave you feeling just dead and unfulfilled — which is all a striptease club does. . . . I'm merely feeling that something has been lost since the days when Aristophanes could write *Lysistrata* which is at the same time funny, accurate, suggestive, and satisfying on the subject of sex. . . .

If a character starts off by being sympathetic and then turns off in a direction that people don't like, that is in fact what often happens with people that one knows in life. I don't understand this assumption that some people have that you have to present the audience with a character that they can identify with. I think that you can identify with any character at any given moment of the play. I never write a scene so that the audience can identify with any particular character. I try and write the scene truthfully from the point of view of each individual character, so that there are obviously episodes in the play in which people will have more sympathy with one character than another. . . .

Sheer propaganda in the theatre is a bore, and completely uncommitted playwriting is also a bore. I think what I'd like to do is to run somewhere between the two, so that one has a point of view, but one doesn't force it on the audience, one merely suggests it at intervals. And you try to see the other side, not out of a sort of wishy-washy liberalism, but simply because if you don't show the other side you aren't giving a true dramatic picture of the personal relationships, which is, after all, what the play is about. . . .

Galileo is a great play because at the end of the play you still don't know where you are. The argument has been presented — was Galileo right to recant his theories on the pressure from the Inquisition, or was he wrong? Galileo himself tells the audience that he was wrong, that he is disgusted with himself. But in the play you actually see the result of his recantation is that he's able to finish the book, smuggle it out of Italy, and it is broadcast all through Europe, while he himself remains alive to do this. Now the point is that you are presented with an action and an argument. They don't reinforce each other. They cross each other, and the one is as strong as the other. . . .

I'm all for intellectual plays, but I think they have definitely a subordinate place. To go back to a remark of Tyrone Guthrie's: 'The theatre is a temple and a brothel'. And it's only a debating hall once it's been these two. In other words, the poetry comes before the rational discussion.

> 'On Comedy: John Arden Talks to Albert Hunt',
> *Encore,* No. 57 (Sept.-Oct. 1965), p.13-19

A Catalyst between the Gods and Men (1963)

I have nothing against good Apollonian drama — I am very fond of *I'm Talking about Jerusalem* [by Arnold Wesker] which is a more or less consistent example of the genre — but it is not my theatre, nor has it been the theatre of tradition in any civilization that I can think of. It is, quite simply, nothing to do with divinity: and as far as I am concerned, the theatre exists to bring the gods down into the bodies of men, i.e., the actors, so that they may be for a few hours *possessed* upon the stage in front of the audience. . . . As a dramatic poet, I see it as my function to act as an intermediary between the gods and the actors, a catalyst if you like, to bring them together.

> 'A Theatre for the Gods', *Peace News,* 25 Oct. 1963

To a Young Dramatist (1964)

For a young dramatist studying his craft, there is no better exemplar in the language than Jonson. He wrote according to the rules and, allowing for certain changes in theatrical practice, they are rules that still hold good. But the matter of his plays is of so dense and knotty a texture and their bitter taste is so difficult to acquire that audiences are more likely to be repelled than seduced by his work. Shakespeare, on the other hand, is practically impossible as a teacher. He follows the classical rules to some extent, but modifies and ignores them at his pleasure until they are scarcely discernible as a structural backbone.

'To a Young Dramatist,' *The Guardian,* 23 Apr. 1964
(For Arden at length on Jonson, see 'Ben Jonson and the Plumbline', in *To Present the Pretence,* p.25-36)

The 'Secret Play' in Henry V (1964)

The *surface* meaning of *Henry V* is certainly that 'Agincourt was a lovely war', and I have no doubt that this was the meaning that Shakespeare intended his audience (and actors) to find in it. But there are so many corrections of this view in the structure of the play that one is forced to wonder if the author had not become prematurely disillusioned with his hero and, while ostensibly following the obvious line laid down by Holinshed, written what is a secret play within the official one. . . . I believe that Shakespeare knew that his more profound ideas about Henry V would never be accepted by his theatre or his audience, and so he concealed them from all but the closest students of the play. . . . This is not an improbable concept — I myself constantly write secret plays within my ostensible ones. Not for political reasons, because nowadays political disillusion is OK in the theatre, but in order to relieve myself of certain personal preoccupations that the dramatic form renders impracticable of communication to an audience.

'Henry V', New Statesman, 19 June 1964 (Arden writes at length on *Henry V* in *To Present the Pretence,* p.197-208)

Theatre in a True State of Socialism (1964)

In what I conceive of as a true state of socialism (by which I mean a society devoted to the health and delight of all of its individual members in every aspect of their personalities) the theatre will serve our mental and sensual satisfaction by presenting us with an image of our common humanity, our fallibility, our greatness, our excitement in the pleasures of the flesh and the potentialities of our spirit and intellect. If this is regarded as a worthy object, then it must be provided for as a public service.

'Theatre and Leisure', *Socialist Commentary,*
Aug. 1964, p.29-31

85

How to Understand Hell (1964)

Today we do not on the whole believe in hell. Our hell is made on earth: we make it ourselves in Auschwitz, at Hiroshima, in the Brig [American military prison], at Hola Camp [prison in Kenya for Mau Mau suspects, 1950s], in Alabama, and so forth.... Plays must examine violence until it is understood and can be controlled.

'How to Understand Hell', *Twentieth Century,*
Winter 1964-65, p.99-101

On Poetic Inspiration (1964)

I am perhaps more interested in a sort of historical or legendary approach to my work.... The Yorkshire countryside and also the Irish countryside, where I sometimes live, is conducive to this type of imagination....

I do believe, to a large extent, in the old idea of inspiration: that the traditional image of the poet being inspired by his muse, as envisaged as a sort of angelic lady whispering in his ear, does have a certain psychological truth; that the things that will make a poem a poem, rather than just a prosaic statement in metrical form, derive from the subconscious and one has to clear one's mind and let them swim up, as it were.

[When Arden feels he is ready to write a poem] I sit down and try and make my mind as blank as possible for a long time in the hope that something will emerge.... I find that I can obtain [a mood] by putting a record by Handel or Bach or Vivaldi on the record-player and becoming involved in a kind of hypnotic state from the rhythms of that music, to which I am very susceptible.

Interview in *The Poet Speaks,* p.1-6

Literature and the Cult of Personality (1965)

Literature generally has been spoiled by the cult of the personality of the individual artist. But Homer, the ballad-tradition, the saga-writers ... they were poets with small *p*s, deliberately impersonal, and unequalled in truth, clarity, and beauty. Compare *Njal's Saga* with *War and Peace.* The Icelandic writer is dealing with enormous political and social problems, matching private themes against public ones, and the style of his work is strictly anonymous. But Tolstoy ... a great writer, of course, but he is always trying to interpret history for us, and his own feelings about Napoleon don't really match up to the size of the war. In the saga, the author was a communal voice, speaking for a whole community;

he reflected the way everyone was thinking. That wasn't possible for Tolstoy nor is it possible for us; society is too complex today. The writer is thrust out on a limb and becomes a kind of prophet.

Your plays indicate that you are particularly interested in politics, is this so?

Yes, but in the dramatic side of politics, in the effect of political crisis on people. I find it hard to get worked up by party programmes, and I couldn't really give any loyalty to either party. I am more interested in what Wilson says to Brown in the Commons tea-room than in any abstractions.

Interview with Benedict Nightingale,
'The Theatre of Bewilderment', *The Guardian,* 6 July 1965

Solving the Political Problem (1966)

Any sort of community drama can at present only work, if at all, on the most modest scale. Miss D'Arcy's experiments have been modest — for anything larger I have had to make use of the professional theatre with all its remoteness, its irrelevance, and its inability to attract a 'popular' audience. This is not a satisfactory situation, but it can't be cured by literature. . . . Until the political problem is solved, I doubt if we shall make much progress with the artistic one. Who's for a revolution?

Interview in *Theatre at Work,* p.57

The Lost Civic Role of Theatre (1968)

Nobody has ever satisfactorily decided 'What the theatre is for'. Aristotle *assumed* that it was one among several functions of the *polis.* He saw it as just another place where the entire voting population of Athens gathered together on matters of public interest: but where, instead of witnessing — and indeed taking part in — the debates and conflicts of their living public men, the population looked on at actors pretending to be the public men of an earlier age (if it was tragedy; if it was comedy, a rude version of today's personalities might be expected). . . . He recognized that the theatre had some sort of subordinate social role to play in the city-state: and the city-state, without theorizing much, clearly recognized this too, or else the plays would not have been put on. Unfortunately for the theatre we no longer live in city-states. We have no public gathering place where Messrs. Wilson or Heath may be confronted by even a small representative selection

87

of the electorate at a time when they are seriously debating policy.
                    'Matters of Public Interest', *Manchester Guardian Weekly*,
                                                        18 July 1968

Professing Drama (1968)

There is no way to interpret the harrowing experiences of the
twentieth (or any other) century in terms of the theatre except
by making plays about them. And there is no way to make plays
which will communicate directly to the public without trying
continually (with a foreseeable failure-rate of approximately 90
per cent) to find some new physical context for their realization
— new, that is, in terms not only of acting-styles and dramaturgy
but also of architecture, publicity and general social relevance. . . .
The view of society from even the most *engagé* university chair is
a little like the view of Setzuan from the gods' cloud in the Brecht
play — extensive; but depressingly astral.
                            'Professing Drama', *The Guardian*, 29 Nov. 1968

The Indian Experience (1971)

A prestige position on a pacifist newspaper [*Peace News*] was, I
came to feel, at any rate for myself, a classic piece of Fence-
Sitting. It enabled me to offer pronouncements upon public
affairs from a position of safety — I could attack governments
and F[orce]s of L[aw] and O[rder] with enthusiasm, while at
the same time avoiding direct action and its consequent peril for
myself by pleading my principles . . . so I quit. I then went to
India. In India the war between the fed men and the hungry men,
the clothed men and the naked men, the sheltered men and the
exposed men, is being waged with great ferocity. . . . Mao Tsetung,
that succinct poet, has said, 'Whatever the enemy opposes, we
must support; whatever the enemy supports, we must oppose'. . . .
I recognize as the enemy the fed man, the clothed man, the
sheltered man, whose food, clothes, and house are obtained at
the expense of the hunger, the nakedness, and the exposure of so
many millions of others.
                        Preface, *Two Autobiographical Plays*, p.13-17

History and Human Potential (1971)

The object of the theatre ought to be to get people to question
society and it should be subversive in the best sense of the word.
It should create in the theatre a vision of society which isn't

available at the moment. One should always be optimistic. If you write a pessimistic play, it should be set in the context that things don't *have* to be bad. There are two things that can be done in the theatre. One is to show people what they are like, or what they have been like. Now this is not normally a very exhilarating experience because human history is full of tragedies and failures. But the other possibility, which isn't perhaps as fully understood as it should be, is that the theatre must show the potentiality of people. It's an expression of energy which throughout our society is muffled and aborted by circumstances over which people apparently have no control.

If you go back into history a little, everything becomes a little easier to handle. It's a reaction against the mass-media view of the world that we get nowadays. If you write a play about Cyprus, it is very difficult to keep all sorts of other things from coming into it — you know, things like the United Nations and the Cold War. If you take the play back to a period in which the British Army was able to do its duty uninhibited by these considerations, then you've got a tighter structure. It could be said that it's shirking the issue a little bit, you know, that you're not reflecting the sophistication of modern life. But I don't think that's what the theatre's supposed to do. I think the place to do that is the cinema.

'John Arden Interviewed by Brendan Hennessy',
Transatlantic Review, No. 40 (Summer 1971), p.52-9

On the Arden-D'Arcy Collaboration (1972)

It is not a question of converting people by the plays but of simply advancing the bounds of theatre. It is converting people to the belief that the theatre may have something to say to them.

I've never regarded myself as anything but a writer. I have never seen myself as a director or political agitator but I've never been satisfied that the writer's role should simply involve sitting behind a typewriter. I've always wanted to be involved with more practical activities without having to initiate them, and so, in that way, our collaboration has enabled me to do a kind of writing which otherwise I would never have done.

The kind of theatre that we do together is very nerve wracking and involves a much closer relationship with the audience and the public at large than writing plays for theatres in London. I think this ought to be done, although I'm not very happy about having to do it. . . . Yet I do think this is a direction in which the theatre ought to go. I probably wouldn't have found myself involved in

this kind of theatre if it had not been for Margaretta D'Arcy.
> Interview with Raymond Gardner, 'Exit, Stage Left',
> *The Guardian,* 28 Nov. 1972

The Complex Craft of the Playwright (1975)

A Play-writer is simply a person who puts pen to paper and sets down dramatic dialogue. But the Playwright pursues an ancient and complex craft analogous to the crafts of the Cartwright, the Millwright, the Shipwright, or — in old Scots — the Wright, pure and simple. The origin of the word is Old England Wyrht = a work, or Wyrcan = to work. The Playwright *works* drama just as the Millwright *works* mill-gear. And working or making a play includes what are now thought to be the activities of the Director *as well as* those of the Script-writer. Such an artist requires a wider workshop than the keyboard of a typewriter. He/She must see him/herself as a person capable of presenting a complete artistic vision upon the stage — not as a semi-skilled sub-contractor to the theatre, who requires someone else actually to produce the play once its text is completed. . . . I joined a profession crippled by generations of exclusion from the workshop-floor — and I found it a grave hindrance at all stages of my career as a Playwright.
> 'Playwrights and Play-Writers', *To Present the Pretence,*
> p.210-11 (from a lecture given in 1975)

The Playwright in Society (1975)

People prefer not to have plays about society, because it worries them. I mean, the fact is that society is in a bad way, and it's always more comforting to see plays that don't go into this, but instead go into the private troubles of the individuals because the audience can identify with those. It may be silly to carry on writing plays like I do, but I do believe that the theatre is a public place, and I do believe that it ought to deal with historical and public issues. I don't believe, anyway, that emotional experiences of individuals are particularly valid if detached from a perspective of the society in which the individuals live, and from the background in which they are formed as individuals.

The more I write, or have written, on the topical Irish themes, the more I feel that I am fulfilling some sort of function in a community, which is something that I was beginning to lack very much when I lived in Britain. There seems to be great possibility for a dramatist to make money and names for himself in Britain, but without being really wanted.

Interview with Maria Kreisler, 'Theatre of Argument
but a Theatre with a Point of View', p.21-3

From Onlooker to Participant (1977)

The actor on the stage pretends: and presents the pretence to the public. To what end, and in what manner, the social conditions of the age and the occasion will determine. 'Look at us', the players imply: 'We are you'. But the spectator well knows that they are also themselves, and they are also the figments of the imagination of the playwright. Their crucial combination of *pretence* and *presentation* gives rise to the strained, almost inhuman posture of the classic theatrical icon – those early nineteenth-century prints of actors in character – 'Mr. Kean as Richard III' – 'Mrs. Siddons as Volumnia' – one arm across the breast, the other stretched out, and the features contorted with apparently immobile passion. When I think of 'the Drama', it is always such an engraving with its crude primary colours and its tinsel embellishments that inevitably comes into my mind.

But to say this is to say nothing of the *content* of plays: what they tell, and to whom. To begin with, I was never very concerned about such things. I found a *story* which appealed to me, for whatever reason, and began to write it, in dialogue: and that was it. About twenty years ago, however, I entered into a working partnership with Margaretta D'Arcy. . . . Her own instincts as a playwright have tended to operate in the reverse order to mine. She will think of a *subject* that requires to be dramatized: and will relate it to the conditions of the time and the potential audience to be sought for it. Only then will the idea of a story to embody the theme, and a style to narrate the story, become uppermost in her mind. The plays I have written by myself and those which she and I have written together are, consequently, quite distinct, one group from the other, in both manner and matter.

Twelve years ago I looked on at people's struggles, and wrote about them for the stage, sympathetically, but as an onlooker. Without consciously intending it, I have become a participant. . . . I write from henceforth in that capacity. It can't be helped.

To Present the Pretence, p.11-12, 158

The World is Polarizing . . . (1977)

Someone wrote about me recently that I was now a dedicated Communist devoted to violence, which is not true. . . . I think

91

the world is polarizing and it is the function of a writer to elucidate what is going on.

Paul Vallely, 'John Arden's One-man War against Authority',
Yorkshire Post, 11 Apr. 1977

'Belonging' in the Theatre (1977)

[In the early 'sixties Arden] was never able to feel that I belonged in the modern theatre. I had some of the best actors and actresses in the country on my cast-lists, and I never got to know any of them very much better than if I had been merely a member of their audiences. The audience themselves came and went and applauded politely enough, but the distance between them in their seats and the play on the stage seemed irreducible. . . . I was troubled by a general lack of warmth, a withdrawn coldness, a too-precisely-defined correctitude of artistic technique which seemed to tell the audience: 'thus far and no further – we are the professionals – actors, director, designer, author – and you are to contemplate the work we choose to show you'. . . . When I was actually writing my scripts I had no such attitude of mind. I regarded myself as preparing a story which would be told to the audience on my behalf by the actors, which would in fact be *me* saying something of interest to a whole crowd of people whom I would have liked to believe my friends.

[Since settling in Ireland at the start of the 'seventies] I have been working consistently at plays and projects which have aroused audience-enthusiasm and involvement to a degree I could not have conceived fifteen years ago.

[*Musgrave, The Workhouse Donkey,* and *Armstrong* are the kinds of script] by which some of us once vainly believed that the whole nature of the theatre could be changed, regardless of its financial and political position within society, and regardless of the then universal isolation of the playwright.

'Preface', *Plays One,* p.5-8

On Radio Drama (1982)

Skilled radio actors can project personalities that have absolutely no resemblance to their own size and shape. It is the author's task to make clear to them, from the size and shape of the words alone exactly what these personalities are to be. . . . You can experience what I find to be the most attractive part of the whole business – the assemblage, in only two or three days (where it would take as many weeks in the theatre), of one's entire fictional creation from the written page to the recorded broadcast. . . . The play comes straight back into your head (from which it originally emerged) and — barring serious misunderstandings and misinterpretations — it comes back more or less as you always hoped that it would. For all the physical distance between yourself and your public, you seem so very much nearer to them than is ever possible in the theatre.

'Plays in the Theatre of the Mind', *Sunday Times*,
22 Aug. 1982

a : Primary Sources

Collections of Plays

Plays: One. London: Eyre Methuen, 1977. [*Serjeant Musgrave's Dance, The Workhouse Donkey,* and *Armstrong's Last Goodnight,* all also published separately.]

Soldier, Soldier and Other Plays. London: Methuen, 1967. [*Wet Fish, When Is a Door not a Door?,* and *Friday's Hiding.*]

Three Plays, introduced by John Russell Taylor. Harmondsworth: Penguin, 1964. [*The Waters of Babylon, Live Like Pigs,* and *The Happy Haven.*]

Two Autobiographical Plays. London: Methuen, 1971. [*Squire Jonathan* and *The Bagman.*]

Articles and Essays

Collection

To Present the Pretence: Essays on the Theatre and its Public. Eyre Methuen, 1977. [17 essays, 1964-77, with five linking sections; referred to below as *TPP.*]

Individual Articles and Essays

'Visitors at the Court', *Encore,* No. 16 (Sept.-Oct. 1958) p.37-9. [Reviews four provincial repertory companies that played at the Royal Court during summer 1968, praising George Munro's *Gay Landscape* and Arnold Wesker's *Chicken Soup with Barley.*]

'Correspondence', *Encore,* No. 20 (May-June 1959), p.41-3. [Important statement on nature of theatre: its purpose is 'a kind of secular Eucharist'; birth-death-rebirth is 'the only poetic theme'; popular theatre has a continuing tradition from Aristophanes to present-day pantomime and music hall.]

'The Reps. and New Plays — a Writer's Viewpoint', *New Theatre Magazine,* Jan. 1960, p.23-6. [Provincial audiences are sometimes more sensible than London ones. 'The artificiality of the stage is one of its most important qualities. . . . . I am pleading for the revival of the Poetic Drama.']

'Telling a True Tale', *The Encore Reader,* ed. Charles
Marowitz, Tom Milne, and Owen Hale (London: Methuen,
1965), p.125-9; reprinted from *Encore,* May-June 1960. [The
basis of English poetry is the ballad, which can bear any content
'from tragedy through satire to straightforward comedy'.]
'A Thoroughly Romantic View', *London Magazine,* VII (July
1960), p.11-15. [Describes how childhood preferences for
ballads and Shakespeare shaped his view of theatre. A writer
should be closely associated with a theatre.]
'The Caretaker', New Theatre Magazine, July 1960, p.29-30.
[Pinter's play shows 'the unexpected strength of family ties
against an intruder' and the verbal patterns are revealing about
the workings of the present-day English mind.]
'Delusions of Grandeur', *Twentieth Century,* CLXIX (Feb. 1961),
p.200-06. [On the type of play and language suited to
television.]
'Johnny Finn', *Twentieth Century,* CLXIX (Feb. 1961), p.220.
[Poem.]
'Verse in the Theatre', *New Theatre Magazine,* Apr. 1961,
p.12-17. Reprinted in *English Dramatic Theories: Twentieth
Century,* ed. Paul Goetsch (Tubingen: Max Niemeyer Verlag,
1972), p.111-18. [Discusses kinds of verse and how to blend
prose and verse, with comments on Pinter, T.S. Eliot, Fry, and
Brecht.]
'Whose Dreams', *New Statesman,* 14 July 1961, p.60. [Poem.]
'Playwrights on Playwriting', Encore, No. 33 (Sept.-Oct. 1961),
p.44-5. [Review of book edited by Toby Cole. Questions the
value of dramatists trying to explain themselves: 'If a good
play is written and performed, it will say within itself what
the writer had in mind to say, and probably a good deal more
besides'.]
'King Log, King Stork', *Time and Tide,* 5 Oct. 1961, p.1648-9.
[Review of *Curtains* by Kenneth Tynan, in comic dialogue
form. Notes influence of Tynan's theatre criticism and the
decision of 'some of us . . . to give up all hope of invariably
pleasing him' and 'instead to swim too fast for him to catch
us'.]
'Why Can't We See It?', *The Sunday Times,* 12 Nov. 1961, p.31.
[Review of text of Fry's *Curtmantle.*]
'Some Thoughts upon Left-Wing Drama', *International Theatre
Annual,* V, ed. Harold Hobson (London: John Calder, 1961),
p.187-96, 201-03. [While young British writers are not
propagandist, they show their views in accepting objectively
'what used to be called the seamy side of life'.]

'A Theatre for the Gods', *Peace News*, 25 Oct. 1963, p.10. [In 'Dionysian' theatre, 'clear, three-dimensional dramatic images' are on the stage, as they are not in much of Ibsen and Wesker. 'Apollonian', intellectual theatre has not been 'the theatre of tradition in any civilization that I can think of'.]

'Shakespeare: To a Young Dramatist', *The Guardian*, 23 Apr. 1964, p.11. [While Shakespeare had 'the ability to see a silk purse in a sow's ear, and the confidence to know that if he could see it he would be able to make others see it, too', Jonson's plays are a better model for a young author.]

'Brecht's Workshop', *The Guardian*, 8 May 1964, p.8. [Review of *Brecht on Theatre*, ed. John Willett. Brecht promotes pleasure and understanding in audiences, but his influence in Britain is limited by his Communism, his prose style, and the heavy demands he makes on actors; reprinted in *TPP*.]

'The Difficulty of Getting Things Done Properly', in *Effective Theatre*, ed. John Russell Brown (London: Methuen, 1969), p.146-8; reprinted from *The Guardian*, 16 May 1964, where the title is 'Tatty Theatre'. [All British theatre suffers from insufficient time for consultation between author, director, and designer, as Arden's experience with the Glasgow production of *Armstrong* showed.]

'Henry V', *New Statesman*, LXVII (19 June 1964), p.946-7. [Letter. Shakespeare hints at an anti-jingoist moral in *Henry V;* similarly 'I myself constantly write secret plays within my ostensible ones . . . in order to relieve myself of certain personal preoccupations that the dramatic form renders impracticable of communication to an audience'.]

'Theatre and Leisure', *Socialist Commentary*, Aug. 1964, p.29-31. [One reason the majority do not go to the theatre is the 'lack of connection between the plays themselves and the realities of life'. In a 'true state of socialism the theatre will serve our mental and sensual satisfaction'.]

'Poetry and Theatre', *Times Literary Supplement*, 6 Aug. 1964, p.705. [Arden agrees with Robert Graves that poetry is essentially 'the personal working-out of the poet's relationship with his Muse,' yet the poet in the playhouse has to do something different from this.]

'Sean O'Casey', *The Observer*, 27 Sept. 1964, p.37. [Letter commenting on critical obituaries. Arden has been 'continuously inspired and excited by the plays'. Reprinted in *TPP*.]

'Armstrong's Last Goodnight', *Encore*, No. 51 (Sept.-Oct. 1964), p.50-2. [Important letter explaining his intentions in the play.]

'The Warren Report', *Peace News,* 30 Oct. 1964, p.11. [Letter
urging scrutiny of the Report because the public should not
'lean upon the easy bosom of the official guardians of good
government'.]

'How Many Schoolgirls Has the Censor Raped?', *Flourish* (Royal
Shakespeare Theatre Club, London) No.2 (1964-65), p.5.
[Complete abolition of censorship would not be harmful.
'Filthy language can be used, by an Aristophanes, a Swift,
or a Lenny Bruce to say something important: when it says
something unimportant, who wants to hear it, particularly
if they have to pay for the privilege?']

'How to Understand Hell', *Twentieth Century,* CLXXIII (Winter
1964-65), p.99-101. [On 'Theatre of Cruelty'. The violence in
medieval religious plays could be accommodated within a
faith, but a post-Christian age has to reconsider it from first
principles, which some artists are doing.]

'Theatre People Reply to Our Enquiry (about Realism)', *World
Theatre,* XIV (Jan. 1965), p.44-5. ['In my own work I have
been trying to explore the problems of freedom and/or order.
This is both a psychological and social theme, and can be
dramatically illustrated in many different ways. . . . Realism
as such does not seem to me to be relevant.']

'The Death of Churchill', *New Statesman,* 29 Jan. 1965, p.148.
[Letter, puzzled at the depth and extent of response to
Churchill's death.]

'Mahagonny', The Listener, 11 Mar. 1965, p.380. [Hostile review
of BBC TV production of the opera by Brecht and Weill. The
theme is how 'liberty and general hedonism are thwarted by
the basic capitalist framework upon which this new society is
based'.]

'Lorca: Stage Poet', *Flourish,* No. 4 (Summer 1965), p.14-15.
[Review of Lorca's *Five Plays.* Praises Lorca for stagecraft and
'the genuine effect of peasant art'. But English actors cannot
'divest themselves of their urban inhibitions and present lyrical
passion with affectation'; reprinted in *TPP.*]

'O'Casey and his Workshop', *Manchester Guardian Weekly,*
17 June 1965, p.10. [Review of *Sean O'Casey − the Man I
Knew,* by Gabriel Fallon.]

'Brecht and the Brass Trade', *The Guardian,* 29 July 1965, p.6.
[Examines Brecht's approach to theatre and the technique
of the Berliner Ensemble.]

'Arden', *Plays and Players,* May 1966, p.8. [Letter commenting
on a critic who suggested that there was no big untapped
audience for dramatists like Arden. Arden asserts the city or

region is important: a London audience is not interested in the North of *The Workhouse Donkey*.]

'A Bond Honoured', *The Times*, 11 June 1966, p.11. [Comments on the critical response to John Osborne's adaptation of Lope de Vega, listing questions (such as in what ways has Osborne altered the original) reviewers should have considered, but did not.]

'A First Class Texas Job', *Peace News*, 7 Oct. 1966, p.1-3. [Long reviews of *Rush to Judgement*, by Mark Lane, and *Inquest*, by E.J. Epstein, two critiques of the Warren Commission's findings on the Kennedy assassination; reprinted in *TPP*.]

'Angry Old Man', *Manchester Guardian Weekly*, 26 Jan. 1967, p.11. [Review of *Blasts and Benedictions*, by Sean O'Casey. O'Casey reinvented an Elizabethan-cum-Brechtian kind of play, combining fun with a social purpose.]

'Personal Comment', *Peace News*, 14 Apr. 1967, 12 May, 9 June, 7 July, 18 Aug., 15 Sept., 13 Oct., 10 Nov., 8 Dec., 22 Dec.; 19 Jan. 1968, 16 Feb., 15 Mar. p.3, 12 Apr. p.14, 10 May, 7 June, 5 July, p.3, 2 Aug. p.6, 30 Aug. p.7, 27 Sept. p.7, 25 Oct. p.7, 22 Nov. p.8, 20 Dec. p.2; 24 Jan. 1969, p.6, 21 Feb. p.3, 23 May p.11, 1 Aug. p.2, 5 Sept. p.6: all on p.10 except where noted otherwise. [Series of diary comments on his experiences and on current affairs. The first three deal with impressions of the United States. Especially interesting is that of 13 Oct. 1967, discussing the movies *Bonnie and Clyde* and *The Gospel According to St. Matthew* in terms of commitment. Seven reprinted in *TPP*.]

'John Arden's N.Y. War', *Flourish*, No. 9 (Summer 1967), p.1, 8-9, 16. [A third-person account in *Time-Magazine* style, of his Vietnam play at New York University; reprinted in *TPP*.]

Letter quoted in *Banned! A Review of Theatrical Censorship in Britain*, by Richard Findlater (London: MacGibbon and Kee, 1967), p.180-1. [Outlines some experiences with the Lord Chamberlain's censorship.]

'A Dramatist's Chance', *The Times*, 10 Apr. 1968, p.11. [Letter attacking Lord Chamberlain's ban on further performances of *Early Morning* by Edward Bond.]

'Matters of Public Interest', *Manchester Guardian Weekly*, 18 July 1968, p.11. [Review of *The Theory of the Modern Stage*, ed. Eric Bentley.]

'A Viking with No Balls?', *Peace News*, 1 Nov. 1968, p.7. [Review of *William Morris: His Life, Work and Friends*, by Philip Henderson. Also letter on his view of Morris, 29 Nov. 1968, p.7.]

'Drama from the Professorial Chair', *Manchester Guardian
Weekly,* 19 Dec. 1968, p.15. [Review of *Theatre Notebook,
1947-1967,* by Jan Kott.]

'Human Horatio', *Sunday Times,* 9 Mar. 1969, p.57. [Review of
Nelson and the Hamiltons by Jack Russell. Arden gives his
view of Nelson; useful for understanding *The Hero Rises Up.*]

'Foreword', *New Directions,* ed. Peter Burton and John Lane
(London: MacGibbon and Kee, 1970), p.15-17. [Argues for the
value of the amateur in any community and demolishes
arbitrary professional/amateur distinctions.]

'The Chhau Dancers of Purulia', *Drama Review,* No. 50 (Spring
1971), p.65-75. [Describes a group of native dancers in a
remote part of India, commenting on the prospects of this
surviving in a genuine way and on the effect of possible
political changes on such artistic forms; reprinted in *TPP.*]

'Radio Drama', *Plays and Players,* Oct. 1971, p.59. [The BBC's
fear of topical and controversial work is shown by their
rejection of his proposal for a play about Connolly.]

'John Arden: 2', *Plays and Players,* Dec. 1971, p.14. [Comments
on reactions to his article 'Radio Drama', and on current Irish
events.]

'What's Theatre For?' *Performance,* No. 4 (Sept.-Oct. 1972),
p.9-18. [Describes how he came to write *The Ballygombeen
Bequest* and the problems when he adjudicated a student drama
festival in Galway. Theatre must give a voice to deprived
people.]

'An Embarrassment to the Tidy Mind', *Gambit,* No. 22 (1972),
pp.30-6. [On Ben Jonson; reprinted in *TPP.*]

'The Matter of Britain', *Flourish,* No. 3 (1972-73), p.1.
[Introduces *The Island of the Mighty.* The issue also contains
an article by Albert Hunt, an interview with the play's
designers, and some facts about King Arthur.]

'Distorted Meanings at the Aldwych' (letter with Margaretta
D'Arcy), *The Guardian.* 5 Dec. 1972, p.12. [On *The Island
of the Mighty* dispute.]

'The Island of the Mighty' (letters with Margaretta D'Arcy),
The Times, 9 Dec. 1972, p.15, and 16 Dec. 1972, p.13.
[Their view of their protest against the RSC production of the
play.]

'Kongi's Harvest', *New Theatre Magazine,* XII, 2 (1972), p.25-6.
[Review of Wole Soyinka's play.]

'Murderous Angels – the Text', *New Theatre Magazine,* XII, 2
(1972), p.3-4. [Review of Conor Cruise O'Brien's play; in *TPP.*]

'The *Island* Controversy at the Aldwych' (with Margaretta

D'Arcy), *Performance,* Fall 1973, p.11-20. [The Ardens'
side in their dispute, with comment on their experiences at
Davis; reprinted in *TPP.*]

'John Arden', *All Bull,* ed. B.S. Johnson (London: Allison and
Busby, 1973), p.230-42. [Describes his Army experiences.]

'Ecco Hobo Sapiens: O'Casey's Theatre', in *Sean O'Casey: a
Collection of Critical Essays,* ed. Thomas Kilroy (Englewood
Cliffs, N.J.: Prentice-Hall, 1975), p.61-76. [Focus on
'schematic expressionism' in O'Casey's later plays.]

'John Arden Comments', *Contemporary Dramatists,* ed. James
Vinson (London: St Martin's Press, second ed., 1977), p.46-7.
['At the present time the gap between the playwright and the
active life of the theatre seems as wide as it has ever been: and
it shows no signs of closing. . . . The *content* of new plays is
obscured and neutralized by over-emphasis on aesthetic
theatrical form.']

'Censorship and Cultural Consensus' (with D'Arcy), *The British
Media and Ireland* (London: Campaign for Free Speech on
Ireland, 1979), p.48-9. [Examples of direct and indirect
censorship of their work.]

'Rug-Headed Irish Kerns and British Poets', *New Statesman,* 13
July 1979, p.56-7. [John Bale, author of *King Johan,* 'the
father of the modern British theatre', and the poet Spenser
first tapped the 'strange vein of obsessed distressed
uncomprehending hostility' to the Irish which continues
today.]

'Shakespeare: Guilty', *New Statesman,* 10 Aug. 1979, p.199. ['By
neither within the play nor outside it contradicting Richard's
sentiment', Shakespeare in *Richard II* 'becomes its
accomplice'.]

'Unofficial Voices', *New Statesman,* 17 Aug. 1979, p.79.
[London 'alternative' theatre gives some opportunity for
minorities 'to achieve their own theatrical voice'.]

'They Do But Jest', *New Statesman,* 24 Aug. 1979, p.1280-1.
[The subversive in plays is neutralized by production and
location: some recent examples.]

'Margaretta D'Arcy and John Arden Reply to Benedict
Nightingale and Howard Brenton', *New Statesman,* 28 Sept.
1979, p.479-80. [Plays are needed to show 'exactly how to
apply humane concern to the immediate precise problems we
are confronted with day to day.']

'Private and Public Passion', *New Statesman,* 9 Nov. 1979, p.723.
[Review of *I Love: the Story of Vladimir Mayakovsky and Lili
Brik,* by Ann and Samuel Charters.]

'Semiotic Constipation', *New Statesman,* 23 Nov. 1979, p.814-5.

'Inclosure like a Buonaparte', *New Statesman,* 7 Dec. 1979,
  p.903-4. [Review of *A Writer's Britain,* by Margaret Drabble.]

'Impressing the Crew', *New Statesman,* 28 March 1980, p.481-2.
  [Review of four books on language and literature, noting the
  rise of 'a whole new craft-mystery vocabulary'.]

'Tey Love Tee Not', *New Statesman,* 11 Apr. 1980, p.555-6.
  [Review of three books about 'literature and public affairs,
  and how closely do they interact?']

'That Swine Lillywhite', *New Statesman,* 27 June 1980, p.971-2.

'Elizabethan Images', *New Statesman,* 29 Aug. 1980, p.19.
  [Interesting review of *Shakespeare: the Globe and the World,*
  by S. Schoenbaum.]

'Carrying All Before Her', *New Statesman,* 28 Nov. 1980, p.22.
  [Review of *The Kemble Era,* by Linda Kelly, and *Sex and
  Sensibility,* by Jean Hagstrum.]

'Death-Rider', *New Statesman,* 5 Dec. 1980, p.27-8. [On Lorca,
  'a dramatic poet of the first rank who only can exist in English
  in the mind's eye and the mind's ear'.]

'Plays in the Theatre of the Mind', *Sunday Times,* 22 Aug. 1982,
  p.31. [On writing and listening to radio plays.]

'Relevance is Relative', *The Listener,* 18 Aug. 1983, p.29. [On
  the 'safe', simplistic adaptation for Irish television of Thomas
  Flanagan's *The Year of the French.*]

'Why We Should Speak a Lot Louder over Nicaragua', *The
  Guardian,* 18 Apr. 1984, p.12. ['The very right of an
  independent Nicaragua to exist is today in mortal peril.']

Interviews

'Building the Play: an Interview', in *The New British Drama,* ed.
  Henry Popkin (New York: Grove Press, 1964), p.581-606;
  reprinted from *Encore,* July-Aug. 1961; partially reprinted
  also in *Theatre at Work,* ed. Charles Marowitz and Simon
  Trussler (London: Methuen, 1967), p.36-50, with several
  significant omissions, alterations, and transpositions.

Alan Lovell, 'Writers and Television, 2: The Writer's View',
  Contrast (London), 2 (Winter 1962), p.124-33. [Discusses
  his experiences with the two TV plays and the TV adaptation
  of *Musgrave.*]

Irving Wardle, 'Arden Talking about his Way of Writing Plays',
  The Observer, 30 June 1963, p.19.

Frank Cox, 'Arden of Chichester', *Plays and Players,* Aug. 1963,
  p.16-18. [Mainly on *The Workhouse Donkey.*]

Simon Trussler, 'Questions of Expediency', *Plays and Players,*
    July 1965, p.14-15. [Mainly on *Armstrong* and *Left-Handed*
    Liberty.]

Benedict Nightingale, 'The Theatre of Bewilderment', *The*
    Guardian, 6 July 1965, p.7.

Albert Hunt, 'On Comedy: John Arden Talks to Albert Hunt',
    Encore, No. 57 (Sept.-Oct. 1965), p.13-19; reprinted from
    Peace News, 30 Aug. 1963.

Vincent Canby, 'John Arden Says He Hates Labels', *New York*
    Times, 24 Mar. 1966, p.48.

'Who's for a Revolution?: Two Interviews', *Tulane Drama*
    Review, No. 34 (Winter 1966), p.41-53. The first interview,
    with Walter Wager, is partially reprinted in *The Playwrights*
    Speak, ed. Walter Wager (New York: Dell Publishing Co.,
    1967), p.238-68. The second interview, with Simon Trussler, is
    reprinted in *Theatre at Work,* ed. Charles Marowitz and
    Simon Trussler (London: Methuen, 1967), p.50-7, with three
    additions.

Ira Peck, 'Art, Politics, and John Arden', *New York Times,*
    10 Apr. 1966, Sec. 2, p.1, 3.

Peter Orr, *The Poet Speaks* (New York: Barnes and Noble,
    1966), p.1-6.

John Peter, 'Interview', *Sunday Times,* 9 June 1968, p.53.
    [On *Harold Muggins.*]

Raymond Gardner, 'John Arden', *The Guardian,* 19 Dec. 1970,
    p.7. [On his visit to India.]

Brendan Hennessy, 'John Arden: an Interview', *Times*
    Educational Supplement, 9 Apr. 1971, p.19.

Brendan Hennessy, 'John Arden', *Transatlantic Review,* No. 40
    (Summer 1971), p.52-9.

Raymond Gardner, 'Exit, Stage Left', *The Guardian,* 28 Nov.
    1972, p.10.

Pan Gems, 'The Island of the Ardens', *Plays and Players,* Jan.
    1973, p.16-19.

'Playwriting for the Seventies', *Theatre Quarterly,* No. 24
    (1976-77), p.35-74. [Symposium with thirteen other
    playwrights.]

b: Secondary Sources

Full-length Studies

Ronald Hayman, *John Arden*. London: Heinemann, second ed., 1969.

Simon Trussler, *John Arden*. New York: Columbia University Press, 1973.

Albert Hunt, *Arden: a Study of his Plays*. London: Eyre Methuen, 1974.

Glenda Leeming, *John Arden*. Harlow: Longmans for British Council, 1974.

A.M. Aylwin, *Notes on John Arden's Serjeant Musgrave's Dance*. London: Methuen Educational, 1976.

Frances Gray, *John Arden*. London: Macmillan, 1982.

Malcolm Page, *John Arden*. Boston: G.K. Hall/Twayne, 1984.

Articles and Chapters in Books

Victoria Manchester, 'Let's Do Some More Undressing: the 'War Carnival' at New York University', *Educational Theatre Journal,* XIX (Dec. 1967), p.502-10.

Ronald Bryden, *The Unfinished Hero*. London: Faber, 1969, p.96-103. [*Musgrave* and *Workhouse Donkey*.]

John Russell Taylor, *Anger and After*. London: Methuen, revised ed., 1969, p.83-105.

Arthur D. Epstein, 'John Arden's Fun House', *University Review,* XXXVI (June 1970), p.243-51. [*The Happy Haven*.]

Malcolm Page and Virginia Evans, 'Approaches to John Arden's *Squire Jonathan', Modern Drama,* XIII (Feb. 1971), p.360-5.

John Russell Brown, *Theatre Language*. London: Allen Lane, 1972, p. 190-234.

Marcus Tschudin, *A Writers' Theatre: George Devine and the English Stage Company at the Royal Court, 1956-1965*. Bern: Herbert Lang, 1972, p.99-132. [*Musgrave*.]

John Lahr, *'The Island of the Mighty', Plays and Players,* Feb. 1973, p.31-3.

Charles Marowitz, *Confessions of a Counterfeit Critic*. London: Eyre Methuen, 1973, p.68-72. [*Workhouse Donkey*.]

Malcolm Page, 'Some Sources of Arden's *Serjeant Musgrave's Dance', Moderna Sprak,* LVII (1973), p.332-41.

Katherine J. Worth, *Revolutions in Modern English Drama*. London: Bell, 1973, p.126-35.

Ronald Hayman, *The First Thrust.* London: Davis-Poynter, 1975, p.79-82, 88-92. [*Workhouse Donkey* and *Armstrong* at Chichester Festival.]

Andrew Kennedy, *Six Dramatists in Search of a Language.* Cambridge: Cambridge University Press, 1975, p.213-29.

Michael Anderson, *Anger and Detachment.* London: Pitman, 1976, p.50-87.

Paddy Marsh, 'Easter at Liberty Hall', *Theatre Quarterly*, No. 20 (1975-76), p.133-41. [First performance of the *Connolly Show.*]

Brian Stone and Clive Emsley, *Venice Preserved by Thomas Otway/Serjeant Musgrave's Dance, by John Arden.* Milton Keynes: Open University, 1976, p.23-34.

J.W. Lambert, 'The Man in the Black-and-White Suit', *Times Literary Supplement,* 3 Mar. 1978, p.253.

Craig Clinton, 'John Arden: the Promise Unfulfilled', *Modern Drama,* XXI (Mar. 1978), p.47-57.

Redmond O'Hanlon, 'The Theatrical Values of John Arden', *Theatre Research International,* V (1980), p.218-36.

Contemporary Literary Criticism. Detroit: Gale, Vol. VI (1976), p.4-11; Vol. XIII (1980), p.23-30; Vol. XV (1980), p.18-26.

John Ditsky, *The Onstage Christ.* London: Wilson, 1980, p.157-71. [*Musgrave.*]

Wanda Rulewicz, 'Bertold Brecht and John Arden's Drama', *Acta Philologica,* XI (1980), p.83-94.

Samar Attar, *The Intruder in Modern Drama.* Frankfurt: Lang, 1981, p.91-106, 124-35. [*Musgrave* and *Live Like Pigs.*]

John Elsom, *Post-War British Theatre Criticism.* London: Routledge, 1981, p.167-74. [*Armstrong.*]

Julian Hilton, 'The Court and its Favours', in *Contemporary English Drama,* ed. C.W.E. Bigsby (London: Arnold, 1981), p.147-55.

Henry I. Schvey, 'From Paradox to Propaganda: the Plays of John Arden', in *Essays on Contemporary British Drama,* ed. Hedwig Bock and Albert Wertheim (Munich: Max Hueber, 1981), p.47-70.

Benedict Nightingale, *An Introduction to Fifty Modern British Plays.* London: Pan, 1982, p.329-41. [*Musgrave.*]

Redmond O'Hanlon, 'John Arden: Theatre and Commitment', *Crane Bag* (Dublin), VII, I (1983), p.155-61.

Carol Rosen, *Plays of Impasse.* Princeton, N.J.: Princeton University Press, 1983, p.54-72. [*Happy Haven.*]

Reference Sources

Malcolm Page, 'Theatre Checklist No. 7: John Arden',
  Theatrefacts, No. 7 (1975), p.2-13.
Karl-Heinz Stoll, *The New British Drama: a Bibliography with
  Particular Reference to Arden, Bond, Osborne, Pinter, Wesker.*
  Bern: Herbert Lang, 1975, p.9-10, 16-17, 24-7.
Kimball King, *Twenty Modern British Playwrights: a
  Bibliography, 1956 to 1976.* New York: Garland, 1977,
  p.1-26.

DATE DUE			

Arden   221298